WORKING FOR YOURSELF WIT

Also by B. H. Elvy

HOW TO BECOME A CONSULTANT
MARKETING MADE SIMPLE
SALESMANSHIP MADE SIMPLE

Working for Yourself Without Capital

B. H. Elvy

First published 1994 by
THE MACMILLAN PRESS LTD
Houndmills, Basingstoke, Hampshire RG21 2XS
and London
Companies and representatives
throughout the world

ISBN 0–333–60718–X

A catalogue record for this book is available
from the British Library.

Typeset by EXPO Holdings Sdn Bhd

Printed in Great Britain by
Mackays of Chatham PLC
Chatham, Kent

Contents

List of Illustrations

1 You and Your Dilemma

In what has been called the worst economic recession since the thirties, hundreds of thousands of people throughout the country have seen their jobs disappear or their business fail. Losing one's employment is a shock. Even in times of relative prosperity, when the prospect of re-employment is good, the sense of rejection that results from redundancy can have severe emotional effects. When jobs are vanishing every minute, the prospect of joining the ever-lengthening dole queue is devastating.

In this situation, people react in different ways. Some accept the hand they have been dealt and resign themselves to the inevitability of months, maybe years, of being without work. Others seek every opportunity to find work. They apply for every vacancy they see advertised, but with hundreds of others making application for the same job, they know their chances are slim.

What can one do to help oneself?

The obvious alternative to employment is self-employment. Many have taken that route. For a decade or more, national and local government has encouraged what is called the Enterprise Culture. Schemes have been set up to offer advice and assistance to those who opt to work for themselves in small business ventures. Governmental and other agencies offer start-up loans and medium-term facilities to encourage small business growth. Understandably, since public money is involved, those seeking such support have been required to make a financial contribution from their own resources. This was not a serious deterrent during the boom years of the eighties. Most of those concerned were able to find the sum required from personal savings or by re-mortgaging their house properties.

Today, we have a different situation. A lengthy period of high interest rates, resulting in high monthly mortgage repayments, has depleted savings. The housing market, meanwhile, has largely collapsed. For many now experiencing redundancy, the possibility of raising a capital sum to put towards funding a business is minimal.

Yet the problem remains. Where the chance of regaining employment – at least in the short term – is unpredictable, and

1

without the means to raise capital, how best can you provide an income for yourself and your family?

The answer has to be to find a business activity that can be set up without capital.

1.1   SETTING UP IN BUSINESS WITHOUT CAPITAL

Working for oneself is never easy. It demands courage, sustained effort for years ahead and a lot of self-discipline. Self-employed people are under constant pressure. They are responsible for everything that affects their business. Family and social life must frequently be sacrificed in the interests of the businesses. You may imagine that once you are working for yourself, you will be able to choose the number of hours you put in. In fact, the situation is more likely to be the opposite. Until you reach a stage where you can employ others, everything that has to be done in the business will have to be done by you. You will be forced to work far longer hours when working for yourself than anyone is allowed to do in an employed situation.

You may believe that working for yourself will free you from the stress involved in corporate employment because you will not have a boss putting pressure on you. Nothing is less true. You will constantly have to make decisions. Many will involve taking risks. Every day will bring problems and you will not be able to shelve them. If you try to do so you will find that, even during your leisure moments, they will continue to nag you until you find a way to resolve them. And it is not only business-induced stress you will suffer. The demands of the business will take precedence over family and social considerations, creating stressful situations in these areas of your life. In working for yourself you must expect to endure long periods of frustration and disappointment, relieved only occasionally, when things seem to go right for a change.

But it is not all gloom. There is immense personal satisfaction to be gained from even limited success when you know you have achieved it yourself. And the ultimate prize of creating wealth is always there, urging you onwards. There are many who insist that the only way to really make money in the modern world is to work for yourself. It is certainly the only way to gain freedom from the constraints imposed when you work for others. But the price you may have to pay could be high and this is something you need to consider very carefully.

Working for yourself without capital is entirely possible. It limits your choice of options as to the kind of business you can set up. It makes any planned venture even more vulnerable than the majority of business start-ups based on personal capital or borrowed funding. There is, of course, a consolation worth bearing in mind: what you have not got you cannot lose. If you fail – a possibility that cannot be ignored – you do not go down burdened with debt that could take you years to pay off. However, it would be foolhardy to minimise the difficulties you will face if you decide to work for yourself without capital. Furthermore, if you have been unfortunate and lost your job and can see no immediate prospect of finding another, your situation is vastly different from that of a person who voluntarily quits his or her employment in order to start a business. Firstly, your decision is likely to be made under duress. The situation in which you now find yourself is not of your choosing. Secondly, you may not have a great deal of time to decide what to do. Financially, you could be under extreme pressure to do something – anything, in fact – that offers the chance to earn money. Against this, you could be harbouring the thought that decisions taken in haste often are repented later.

It is in an effort to help resolve this dilemma that this book has been written. Merely reading a book, of course, will not get you out of your difficulties. But it may help you to rationalise your thinking about current problems and will suggest ways and means that could lead you towards a better future.

1.2 YOUR PERSONAL CHARACTERISTICS

The contention that you can, without capital resources, make a living working for yourself needs qualification. Many people have succeeded in doing so in the past and others are doing so now. But there are conditions:

1. You must enjoy reasonably good health. Working solo means there will be no one to step in and hold the fort when you

are ill. Unless you can work consistently, your income will not be consistent. Any prolonged period of ill-health could ruin the business.

2. Whatever the nature of the activity you decide to pursue, it should have some appeal to you. The more intrinsically interesting and satisfying the work, the more you will want to do it. Enjoying one's work is the only true recipe for success.

3. You need to be capable of working on your own. Many people find this the most difficult aspect of self-employment. They miss the camaraderie of working alongside others in office or factory. They feel very isolated when faced day after day with only their own company, unrelieved by the companionship and conversation of others.

4. You must be self-motivating. Once again, this is not easy for those who need the encouragement, or the leadership, provided by others, in order to stay on course and get things done.

5. You need a resilient nature. When things go wrong, you will naturally feel frustrated but you will have to bounce back rather than allow yourself to become depressed and dejected.

6. Excessive impulsiveness can be highly detrimental in running a business. More can be achieved by careful forethought and weighing alternative courses of action than by snap decisions.

7. Every business activity involves other people and especially those who will pay for whatever activity you engage in. This means you will have to be able to get along with them. Customers often seem difficult and unreasonable. You have to be capable of making a conscious effort to be accommodating, however unfair a situation may seem to be.

8. Most important of all, you need determination. Having considered all the factors and decided on a course of action, you must steel yourself to pursue it despite obstacles until you have seen it through. Those who are successful in business are tenacious.

If you genuinely believe that you have the personal characteristics to meet these conditions you are in with a chance when it comes to going it alone without financial backing.

There are three basic ingredients normally regarded as necessary for a successful commercial enterprise. These are:

1. The possession of a marketable idea.
2. The ability to develop the idea into a viable business project.
3. The possession of the necessary resources with which to launch the business.

How a business idea should be developed into a viable project will be discussed in later chapters. So far as *financial* resources are concerned, on the assumption that you do not possess any capital for investment, this criterion is not going to be met. Facilities at your disposal will be those already in your possession and those that can be borrowed or hired at very nominal cost, and we shall consider these later. For the moment, let us consider what is involved in finding a marketable – and suitable – idea that could enable you to start your own business.

1.3 ADOPTING A NEW OUTLOOK

In the circumstances in which you are placed, this is unlikely to be easy or straightforward. It may well be necessary for you to adopt an entirely new outlook on life. One of the most harrowing aspects of losing one's job is coming to terms with an abrupt change of lifestyle. We are all creatures of habit. Habitual surroundings and activities, the daily routine of going to and from our places of work, the detail of the tasks we perform, the companionship of people we understand and are comfortable working with: these are often the sentinels that guard our sense of security. When redundancy strikes, suddenly they are gone. Relationships are severed. We are no longer needed. The pattern of our working lives is destroyed. It is as if an abyss opens at our feet and we stare at it in disbelief.

A natural reaction is to think it a mere aberration, just a temporary setback. Surely another job must be waiting for us, round the corner? Very soon, we shall pick up the threads of normality, and life as we have always known it will resume its course. The brutal fact that the familiar life-style that we have taken for granted has finished for ever can be almost impossible to accept.

Yet accept it one must, in order to be free of the past and to prepare for the future.

The first and most important thing you must do is to consider your assets. They may be many, or few, according to your individual circumstances. Whatever your personal situation, however, you have one priceless asset: your ability to think. Thinking will cost you nothing. Your mind is your best resource and the more you exercise it the better it will perform.

Few people think purposefully. Most of our thinking tends to be reactive. Our minds spontaneously react to situations as they arise. We are all liable to day-dream, of course. We conjure thoughts about largely improbable events or situations and indulge our imagination as to how we like to think we would deal with them. But none of this is purposeful thinking.

Purposeful thinking needs an objective. The objective of your thinking at this juncture should be how you will handle the trauma of losing your job and how you will find the means of working for yourself without capital. Your thinking must be positive. Negative thoughts about the possible causes that led to your redundancy – whether you should have jumped out of your job before you were pushed and found another while the employment situation was easier – will gain you nothing. Nor should you dwell on the negative aspects of your current situation. Of course, it is bad! But you already know that. Working out in your mind just how bad it is will only delay your recovery by preventing you from thinking about your future.

Every situation has a positive as well as a negative aspect. The working life-style you have lost doubtless had its advantages. But was it totally rewarding? Chance plays a vital part in dictating the course of our lives and few people, looking back to their youth, can say that they deliberately chose the career path they subsequently followed. There is a positive side to redundancy because, unbidden though it is and without any desire to minimise the misery it often brings, it does provide the opportunity for a fresh start in life. If you can fasten on to this aspect of your present situation, thinking in terms of advantages – rather than the disadvantages that are patently obvious and need no further repetition – you can put your mind to where you want to go from here.

Let us look at some of the positive aspects of life after redundancy. For the first time in many years you no longer go to work each day. This means that, with commuting time included, you have at least fifty hours a week at your disposal. Throw in only half of your former leisure hours and you have around seventy hours every week to do whatever it is you decide to do. Furthermore, during all those years you were employed, did you never think you would *prefer* to do something different to the work you were being paid to do? You would probably never have seriously contemplated giving up a secure job to take on a different role; but now you *can* consider what you would like to do.

Most people are prisoners of their past. They are mentally conditioned to think of themselves as confined within a particular category: salesmen or engineers; accountants or draughtsmen. Their minds are closed to the possibility of changing their roles. Many are inhibited in their thinking by social convention. The so-called white-collar worker cannot imagine himself undertaking an artisan occupation. But the clerical worker who rolls up his sleeves to do manual rather than mental work is no less a person simply because he gets his hands dirty. Indeed, he may well find his earnings substantially increased! The new freedom that accompanies redundancy provides the opportunity to widen your vision because the limitations imposed by your former working life-style no longer apply.

In order to think purposefully about how you will achieve your objectives, consider basic factors and try to draw reasonable assumptions from them. Examine your personal capabilities. You need to take account of your strengths and of your weaknesses. This will enable you to set limits as to what you may or may not be able to do.

1.4 YOUR PERSONAL CAPABILITIES

The best way to do this is to take a few sheets of paper, choose a time and place in which you will not be interrupted and think about yourself and everything you have going for you. Make notes as you do so. Here are a few pointers, to help you get started:

1. What do you know about?
2. What are you particularly good at doing?
3. What experience have you got?
4. What contacts do you have, in business and socially, that could possibly be of any help to you?
5. What facilities do you have, should you decide to run a business from home? Spare room, garage, workshop, shed?
6. Do you have a car?
7. Do you have any tools or specialised equipment that could be used in a business?
8. Are there members of your immediate family who could help you in running a business? Do they have any special skills, knowledge, experience or contacts that could be helpful to you?

Write down whatever comes to mind, as it comes. The trick is to let the mind flow freely. Your aim should be to set down a brief note of every conceivable plus that you can think of drawn from your past experiences. Hobbies, sports, interests, anything you have done which you remember you did rather well, should go down on your list. Once you have drained your mind of your pluses, take another sheet of paper. This time, list the things you are not good at. Be honest with yourself and set down your shortcomings, the things you dislike having to do. Include your areas of ignorance, too. Activities of which you have little or no knowledge are not necessarily matters you could not tackle if you set your mind to it; but your ignorance of them will suggest that they have no appeal to you.

The value of doing this personal audit of strengths and weaknesses is that it will help you to define those sectors of business activity most suited to your own capabilities. It will help narrow the field in your search for a viable business activity. A factor not to be overlooked, in view of your lack of capital, is that certain areas of business are closed to you. For example, most forms of manufacture involve the purchase of equipment and materials before production can commence. A trading operation requires the purchase of stock. Many industrial and commercial activities can only be carried on in purpose-built factories or retail shops, putting them outside your range. The

principal area of business activity that is open to you is the provision of a service.

The service industry has grown enormously in the past twenty
years. As people generally have become better-off, many of the
tasks they once did for themselves they now pay others to do for
them. Business companies of all kinds now find it more economical to buy-in certain services, such as office-cleaning, the maintenance and repair of office equipment, accountancy and
secretarial services, rather than carry people on their payrolls to
perform such tasks.

When thinking about the type of activity to pursue, there are
two alternative courses you can follow. One is to imitate what
others are already doing. The other is to innovate. Whilst there
have been some very successful businesses built on the exploita-
tion of a novel idea, it is generally advisable to avoid speculation
on a form of service no one has attempted before. This is
because, where a project is entirely new, no market exists to provide any kind of pattern. You have to create the market yourself.
Customers not only have to be found: they have to be educated
to understand the reasons why they should use the service. To
do this requires a lot of advertising and other forms of promotion, none of which you will be able to afford. Another consideration is that, if the idea is such a good one, why has no one else
thought of it and set up a business to exploit it? It is far better to
stick to well-trodden paths and to provide not a new but a better
kind of service than that currently on offer.

There are some further points worth considering at this stage.
A frequently heard cry from those casting about for a business
idea is that a particular service they would like to perform is
already being supplied by established firms. If one accepted the
argument and took it to its logical conclusion, there would
never be any new businesses coming in to compete with the old.
Unless the market is completely saturated there is always room
for one more. As we shall see when we come to examine markets, these are always in a state of change. If you were to find, for
example, from a cursory glance around your particular locality,
that there was a considerable number of freelance hairdressers
operating, this would not necessarily mean the market was saturated. Where there is competition, there is a market. How you

enter a market an establish yourself alongside your competitors we shall discuss later.

Before leaving the subject, however, it is worth bearing in mind that, to compete with others already established in a particular field, one's performance does not have to be superlative. You need to be as good as your competitors. If you can perform better than they do, eventually you will become more successful than them. The quality of much service provision is low. You must know this from your personal experience. As a nation, all too often we accept low standards and as a result a lot of complacency exists in businesses, large and small, throughout the country. It is this factor that provides opportunity, even for those without start-up capital, to earn a living by working for themselves within the services industry.

1.5   SEEKING YOUR OPPORTUNITY

It is widely recognised that the purpose of any business should be to exploit an opportunity. But there is often doubt as to what constitutes a business opportunity, how such a circumstance is recognised and what needs to be done to take advantage of it.

An opportunity is a favourable concurrence of events taking place at a particular point in time. Put into a commercial context, this means that:

1.   a need is seen to exist;
2.   no one appears currently to be satisfying this need;
3.   you have the means to satisfy it.

In order to discover and exploit an opportunity, it is necessary to understand what is meant by these constituents.

A need seen to exist
All business activity is related to the supply of goods or services to satisfy human wants. At the dawn of history, such wants were basic: food, drink, clothing, shelter. We have come a long way. Today, our wants list extends to many thousands of items. This has been brought about by two major factors: the advance of technology and a concurrent increase in our personal expecta-

tions. Throughout history, yesterday's luxury became today's necessity. But, over time, our perception of wants has varied constantly. Changed circumstances always have been the cause of changed needs and the process never stops. The pattern of our perceived needs ten years hence will differ considerably from that of today. It will result from changes that will occur during the next decade in the way we think and the way we live.

This constant tendency for change is not, however, necessarily uniform. Where the circumstances that have given rise to a particular human need have remained largely stable for a relatively long period of time, an equally stable supply system is likely to be in operation to satisfy it. Scope for a newcomer to enter that supply chain will, at best, be limited. But introduce change to the circumstances and you introduce disturbance to the precise nature of the human need. However satisfying the former provision system, this may not, in the new circumstances, remain fully acceptable.

What this amounts to is that, in order to discover new needs requiring satisfaction, one must look for changing circumstances. These occur in our lives almost every day, in one aspect or another. Usually, we are not immediately aware of them. Only over a period of time does it occur to us that certain circumstances affecting our lives have altered.

When searching for a marketable idea, be alert to change because therein may lie the kind of opportunity you could exploit.

A need not currently satisfied

Recognition of the existence of a need, though the vital first step, does not necessarily provide you with an opportunity. In our competitive society, you are likely to be but one among many to make the same discovery. Whenever you spy what appears to be a new need in your locality, the chances are that someone else will forestall you by moving in first to satisfy it. This does not mean you are excluded from following suit, merely that you have a competitor. Indeed, as mentioned earlier, if you do stumble across what you imagine to be a need and believe this to be your golden opportunity because there is not a competitor in sight, you would do well to question whether the need really does exist. The history of commercial innovation is littered with the corpses of bright ideas that never got off the ground because the need for them was insufficient to make them viable propositions. The existence of a competitor, if he is a successful one, is assurance that a healthy demand prevails.

Despite this obvious need for caution, however, you may find that, for perfectly valid reasons, there is what the pundits call 'a gap in the market'.

To understand how this can come about, it is necessary to recognise the revolution that has occurred in the economic circumstances of this country and of many others in the Western world. The increased level of income that has enabled people generally to seek the supply of services has also vastly increased the cost of providing those services. This is because service industries are heavily dependent on human providers, far more so than manufacturing industries, where mechanisation reduces the need for human labour. The labour-cost element in providing a service is thus crucial to the viability of the operation. As a result, suppliers have become increasingly selective as to the markets and the localities where services can be provided. Unless the volume of business available is sufficiently large to enable them to absorb the cost of paying people to provide it, they can no longer afford to make the service available.

Having the means to satisfy it

Your discovery of a need that is not already being met may well offer you an opportunity. Whether or not it is an opportunity that *you* can exploit, however, depends on the means at your disposal. The audit you have carried out of your personal strengths and weaknesses will have indicated the kind of activity most suited to your capabilities. We have also noted that there are areas of business you must rule out because they require capital investment. Your field of choice, therefore, now begins to narrow. This is necessary and desirable. It makes it easier to define the *type* of opportunity you should be looking for. Despite the constraints imposed by your lack of capital, the business options available to you are numerous and varied, as we shall discover in the next chapter.

2 Consider the Options

When considering possible options as to the type of business activity you will pursue, keep the following conditions in mind.

1. You need to get some intrinsic satisfaction from carrying out the actual work. Making money is a prime consideration but not the only one. You will be working under pressure. You will have many anxieties. Inevitably, there will be times when you will wonder if it is all worth while. At least choose something that you will like doing. That way, the accompanying burdens will be easier to bear.
2. You must be realistic in your choice. Relate your personal capabilities and the resources available to you to what the nature of the work will demand. It is all very well accepting a challenge and being prepared to adapt oneself sufficiently in order to do so. A willingness to stretch oneself is admirable. But to take on a commitment beyond your capacity would be folly.
3. You should not ignore the legitimate claims others may have on you and on your time. Some disruption to current domestic arrangements, and the need for a degree of sacrifice on the part of your family, may be inevitable if you are to work for yourself. But these will create pressures, additional to those you will incur in running the business. Be mindful of such dangers when choosing your activity and recognise the possible effect these could have on those you care for.

On the following pages, there are a number of business options that can be undertaken without capital investment. They cover a wide spectrum and, for the purposes of convenience, have been classified as follows:

2.1 Activities that can be conducted mainly from home. Travel needs will be minor and, if you do not have the use of a car, can be met by public transport.

13

2.2 Activities that will be conducted mainly on customers' premises. These will involve a moderate amount of travel for which a car is likely to be desirable.

2.3 Activities that will require considerable travel, making possession of a car essential. It may also be necessary to spend time away from home several days per week.

2.1 OPTIONS INVOLVING MINIMAL TRAVELLING

Book-finding

There are always a large number of people who, for research purposes or merely their own pleasure, are anxious to obtain copies of out-of-print books which are unobtainable from normal booksellers. If you can set up a book-finding service to meet their needs, you have the makings of a financially rewarding and interesting business. To launch such a venture, you will need to have among your circle of acquaintances people who buy such books and from whom you can obtain leads to others who could also be interested in your service. The alternative is to advertise in publications such as *Books and Bookmen* and those appealing to special interest readers, including *History Today* and the *Geographical Magazine.*

This will, however, involve greater financial outlay than you may wish to incur initially. Using the direct mail method, you could, more cheaply, publicise your service by writing to individual college and university lecturers and other academics who will represent a good source of potential customers for your business. You will need to conduct some market research to prepare a mailing list of appropriate names. Furthermore, if you are located within reasonable distance of such institutions, it may be possible to get your business card displayed on college or university notice-boards.

It would be desirable to specialise initially in subjects or groups of subjects that interest you personally and of which you have some knowledge: history and archaeology or geography and travel; natural history; nautical and marine; for example. There are second-hand booksellers throughout the country and many of them specialise in particular subjects. The Booksellers Association will be able to provide you with the names of many of them. Circulate to them your 'wants' list of books, having ascertained from your customer, wherever possible, details of author and title, the name of the publisher and the date of publication. The service thus provided to your customers will be highly individual, saving them a great amount of time and effort. This should enable you to sell-on the books you obtain at top prices, providing a high margin of profit.

Business appointments booking

Business executives employed by companies, especially those whose work requires them to travel extensively, usually have the advantage of secretaries to book their future appointments. Freelance business people, however, often do not have this facility. This means they must allocate several hours per week or month from their limited working time to arrange their future itineraries. You can relieve them of this problem by setting up an appointments booking agency. By taking on a number of clients and working efficiently with a good telephone manner, you have the opportunity to create a viable business. Ideally, in addition to a telephone, you should have the use of a typewriter and be a moderate typist. You can then confirm your clients' appointments by letter to their contacts, providing copies to the individual clients concerned. To have the use of a fax machine, while not essential, would be an advantage.

Your fees should be based either on the number of appointments booked or on an hourly basis, plus the telephone and postage expenses incurred. If you are fluent in foreign languages, your service could be invaluable to those solo business people involved in import or export activities and this extra facility should be reflected in your charges.

Business history

Business firms recognise the importance of having a good company image. It can be of immeasurable help in their purchasing as well as their sales activities; it assists their recruitment of staff and is often a valuable influencing factor in attracting finance for future expansion. If you can write in an interesting style and have some experience of historical research, you can earn money from business history. The story of a business is to be found in the pages of its minute books and ledgers. You will need to know how to decipher them. You will also need a background knowledge of the particular trade or industry in which a client company has operated down the years. You should study the methods of business history research and here the Historical Association should be able to assist you.

Your market will lie among medium and small-size firms – large organisations tend to use only established writers – and they do not have to be centuries old. The story of a firm that has traded for 25–30 years can be equally absorbing and, very often, the events and personalities involved have greater relevance for readers.

A business history is usually published by and at the expense of the company concerned. An inclusive fee is paid to the author, taking account of time spent in research as well as the actual writing of the book. As finally presented, the script will have to satisfy the client's needs, so it is important to have a clear understanding of what he expects from the outset. Does he want a 'warts and all' exposition of the company's past or are there aspects of its history he would prefer that you gloss over? To what extent will it be acceptable for you to discuss personalities in other than a favourable light? Company history ultimately is about the people who have worked in the firm from its inception to the present day. By revealing their ideosyncrasies and the clashes that may have occurred between them, you enliven the tale and produce a chronicle that makes interesting reading.

Buying and selling

At first glance, this may seem a highly doubtful activity for those without capital. But many successful entrepreneurs have started trading businesses without financial resources. What most of them have possessed, is knowledge of the particular trade or industry in which they began their operations. The way in which one trades without capital is to sell before one buys.

If you were to contemplate working for yourself by such means, it would be essential to have contacts among purchasers from whom to obtain details of their needs. It is then necessary to discover appropriate sources of supply, negotiate acceptable prices and trading terms and obtain an option to purchase. Before expiration of the option, you will need to negotiate a resale price with the potential customer. Having secured the sales contract, you will then conclude a purchase contract with your supplier.

The crux of such a deal is to ensure that you receive payment for the goods from the customer before you are required to settle your account with the supplier. Obviously, in addition to negotiating skills, you will need to have faith in the customer abiding by his undertaking to make payment to you when promised. This type of commercial operation demands considerable mental dexterity and a willingness to take calculated risks. A further essential qualification is a personal reputation for integrity and reliability. It is not the type of business for the faint-hearted. In many commodity markets, however, there are successful dealers operating this so-called back-to-back method on a daily basis. Such transactions are based largely on mutual trust between the parties and, for those with the stomach for it, it is a form of trading that can be highly lucrative. The need for extensive travel is not as great as one might imagine, providing one's relationship with customers is deep-rooted and reliable. Much of the purchasing and selling operations can be conducted by telephone, fax and telex.

Credit controlling

With the exception of retail traders, whose customer transactions are conducted on a cash basis and payment is received at the time of purchase, most firms have to provide credit facilities for their clients. To ensure that these are not abused and that debtors pay in accordance with agreed terms, the exercise of some form of credit control is necessary.

Medium and large size companies usually have credit control departments to handle this function. In the majority of small businesses, however, the task often falls to one of the principals and gets done as and when there is time available or when money suddenly is desperately needed. This is never a satisfactory arrangement.

Debtors frequently need prodding to ensure that payment is made when due and renowned slow-payers must be chased frequently if their accounts are to be kept reasonably up-to-date. The failure of a business to get in the money it is owed can create dangerous cash-flow problems and put the entire enterprise at risk. Debtor payment-chasing is work that can be done in one's own home, using the telephone.

If you should decide to take up this activity, you should have a good telephone manner and be able to adopt a courteous yet firm attitude towards your clients' customers. Your objective will be to secure prompt settlement of due and overdue accounts without giving offence to the firms concerned, because your clients will wish to retain them as their customers for the future.

In situations where customers place orders on a regular month-by-month basis with client firms, the task of ensuring that their payments, too, are made regularly, will involve a recurring dialogue with the individuals responsible for making such payments. Where a degree of accord is established between the two of you and a sensible understanding of mutual problems results, the work is not onerous.

Many small businesses find it preferable to farm the chasing of payment from customers to an outside agency, rather than use their own staff, particularly if it is the task of those who would be concerned also to sell to those customers. You will need to be well organised. You should keep notes of conversations and the promises of payment obtained from those you chase. This is for your own benefit when making follow-up calls and also enables you to keep your clients informed of the ongoing situation.

Your fees should be based on an hourly rate plus telephone expenses. The number of individual clients you will be able to accommodate will depend on the total number of customers to be contacted on a regular basis. Calls to firms can only be made during normal business hours and, where the individual you need to contact is heavily involved in production or sales matters, he or she may often be genuinely unavailable. This may require a series of re-calls to make the required contact.

Dressmaking and knitting

Bespoke dressmaking and hand knitting are traditional home-work activities and for those skilled in such work provide a ready source of income. For even the fastest of workers, however, the achievable rate of output will severely limit earnings unless one produces garments for an up-market, affluent and discriminating clientele.

Investment in a sewing or knitting machine, if it can be afforded, may enable you to sell to local boutiques or shops specialising in maternity or baby-wear. Apart from possessing sewing or knitting skills, you will need to keep abreast of fashion trends and, if a dressmaker, a knowledge of fabrics will be important. Ultimately, where you live and your proximity to an area containing a sufficient number of potential clients willing and able to spend money on individually produced garments, will be the deciding factor as to whether you can establish a successful business.

Guest house keeping

For those living in popular tourist centres, using one's home as a guest house was, at one time, a means of earning money without major investment. The situation is different today. Legislation has imposed restrictions, ranging from the percentage of rooms in the house that you are permitted to let to guests, to the provision of fire exits, observance of local planning requirements and conformity to environmental health laws and hygiene regulations.

Before involving yourself in this type of activity, discuss your ideas with your local tourist authorities and invest in a guide published by the English Tourist Board, called: *Starting a Bed and Breakfast Business*. It is sponsored by Barclays Bank and describes the day-to-day operation of a venture of this kind.

Home baking

Despite the dominance of factory-produced foods served in pubs and hotels, there is considerable scope for the sale of home-baked pies, pâtés and similar items to speciality food shops and to wine bars seeking to offer more distinctive dishes to their clientele. If you have a particular flair for this kind of home cooking, here is an opportunity to create a lucrative business.

Research your local market, bearing in mind that the price at which items of this nature are sold to the public often contain a profit margin to the retailer of fifty per cent of more compared to the price he has paid to the producer. Remember that preparation of food at home for sale requires you to observe the statutory hygiene regulations, copies of which you should obtain from HMSO. You should also inform your local environmental health inspector and your local planning officer of your intentions before you start trading.

Fancy dress hiring

For those with dressmaking skills, flair and imagination, the considerable market that exists for fancy dress hire affords an opportunity to earn money. The materials one works with can often be obtained cheaply. Second-hand garments, unpicked and possibly dyed, can be refashioned into fancy dress costumes, often at minimal cost.

This is the sort of business that can be run from your own home, providing you have a suitable workroom equipped with mirrors and screening for a changing area. Once started, it should not take too long to build up a considerable stock of garments, including those that you make yourself or adapt, as well as ready-made costumes you may be able to buy second-hand. There are fashion trends in fancy dress as in all forms of apparel and it will be important to keep yourself informed of the changing needs of your market.

House history researching

People moving into houses built a hundred or more years ago often have a natural curiosity about their predecessors. In many old properties, they are likely to find evidence of structural alterations, undertaken long ago, and they wonder about the appearance and layout of the house when it was originally built. The compiling of a house history has become an increasingly popular service in up-market districts where the homeowners enjoy a considerable disposable income.

To provide it, you need to have some understanding of the methods of historical research, coupled with a knowledge of architectural principles and design. These are subjects that you can read up, using your local public library. Apart from property owners, local firms of estate agents are also potential clients. When handling the sale of country houses, for example, they often produce quality illustrated publicity brochures that extol the virtues of the property. They could well be interested in the inclusion of brief histories of such houses.

Fees, plus expenses, charged to homeowners should be based on an hourly rate and will vary in accordance with the amount of research that has to be undertaken. The abridged pieces you supply to estate agents should be charged at an inclusive fee.

A possible by-product of your researches could be the writing of articles regarding local houses for publication in county magazines and in promotional literature published by your local tourist board. Prior to doing so, however, it may be advisable to obtain the consent of the homeowners who originally commissioned and paid for your research. Some researchers cover this point by writing into the agreement they reach with the homeowner a clause clarifying who will have title to the information obtained from the research.

Importing–exporting

With a business background and connections in a particular sector of trade or industry, there is an opportunity to make money operating an import–export agency. You will need telex and fax facilities although, initially, you may be able to have the use of these through a business friend on a temporary basis, until your agency is established.

This kind of activity does not require a licence and you do not have to have specific qualifications. What you do need are contacts, either in the home market or abroad – preferably both. Your task will be to identify firms seeking supplies of particular products and then to find appropriate sources. Depending upon which party has the greater need for your services, you can either take a selling or a buying commission. Providing you deal only with reputable organisations and have an understanding of the trade or industry concerned, your operating risks are minimal. You should, however, make yourself fully conversant with the detail of import–export procedure and with customs regulations. The British Overseas Trade Board will supply to you, free of charge, a wealth of information on these subjects.

Mailing list broking

Direct mail now plays a major role in the marketing of goods and services of all kinds. The foundation of any direct mail campaign is the list of names and addresses of private individuals or business firms it is proposed to canvass. The number of available lists has become bewildering and companies preparing to run campaigns look increasingly to list-brokers to find those most appropriate to their particular needs.

To become a direct mail list-broker you will need at least a background knowledge of the subject in order to provide a suitable service, plus plenty of contacts. You will work on a commission based on the list owner's rental fee and, by specialising in the provision of lists related to particular market segments, it should be possible to build a viable business.

You must, however, be familiar with the requirements of the Data Protection Act and it would be advisable to get in touch with the regulatory body, which is the British List Brokers' Association. Setting up a list-broking agency, which can be run from home, should not involve much outlay. In due course, a computer and a database will prove invaluable but these are not essential at the outset.

Model-making

Many people enjoy model-making as a hobby. To do so professionally requires considerable skill, often combined with architectural or mechanical knowledge. The market for bespoke model making is perhaps more varied than might at first be apparent. In addition to architect practices and planning authorities, you may well find work among industrial firms seeking working models to illustrate new processing equipment and among marketing organisations wanting novel display items. As with most highly specialised activities, there is a scarcity factor that should enable you to attract very good prices for your work. This kind of business grows mainly through recommendation, and promotional costs, once a nucleus of initial clients has been established, are likely to be minimal.

Nursery equipment hiring

A somewhat unusual but nonetheless viable business is the hiring out of nursery equipment. There is a constant demand for prams, travel cots, children's buggies, play-pens and all the other paraphernalia so necessary to families with very young children. The cost of such items bought new can place a big strain on the budgets of young families. Hence the popularity of a service that provides such equipment on a hire basis.

Some agencies supply only top-of-the-range equipment which they purchase brand new. Others mostly buy second-hand items, provided they are in good condition. Hire periods usually are six to twelve months. Short-term arrangements, however, are often available to suit special needs, such as those of grandparents with families visiting at Christmas or on other holiday occasions.

Without available capital to purchase new equipment, you should find it possible to pick up discarded nursery items for a minimum outlay among friends and acquaintances and by putting cards in newsagents' windows. This is how many others have managed to start such hire agencies without much financial outlay, going on to replace old equipment with new as and when sufficient funds have become available.

Performers' diary-keeping

This is a decidedly off-beat, yet financially viable, proposition for those with sufficient tenacity and imagination. Freelance performing artists of all kinds, especially musicians, are faced with a constant problem: while away from home, fulfilling current engagements, they are missing the opportunity of future work simply because those seeking to employ them cannot contact them promptly.

Relatively few orchestras are in a position these days to place players on contract. With a limited number of concerts taking place annually, managers are forced to 'ring round', often at short notice, in order to book suitable instrumentalists. If they fail to reach the individuals they prefer they engage alternative players instead. However, where performers subscribe to a diary service, they can leave an answerphone message directing callers to contact the diary-keeper in their absence. The diary-keeper, previously informed of the player's present whereabouts, can then inform him or her of the future engagement on offer.

To run such a service, one must be prepared to man the telephone throughout the daytime and late into the evening. There will doubtless be occasions when clients will be difficult to track down. Although the diary may indicate where they are staying and the particular hall or theatre where they are playing, one faces the possibility of their being unobtainable at the very time their decision on a forthcoming engagement is urgently needed.

Musicians are not, of course, the only performers who can benefit from such a service. If such a venture appeals to you, you will need a nucleus of contacts among performers to create an initial client base. Since competition is likely to be extremely slight, your fees for the service can be as much as the market will bear. But keep in mind that, although your start-up costs could be virtually negligible, you will inevitably run up very high telephone bills when contacting clients over long distances.

Playgroup leadership

The numbers of young mothers entering full or part-time employment to assist the family finances has created the need for more playgroups to care for pre-school-age children. Many are run on a small scale by individual women in their own homes, perhaps assisted by a friend or relative. Others cater for larger numbers of children, and public halls and similar premises are hired for the purpose.

If such work attracts you, contact the Pre-School Playgroup Association. They will be able to provide you with information and advice. Before you decide to form a playgroup, you should first get in touch with the Social Services Department of your local authority. You must register with them before you can legally proceed. They will need to vet both you and the venue where you intend to operate to ensure suitability. If you decide to operate in your own home, the premises will require inspection and approval by the local Fire Officer and you will also have to obtain planning consent. Much will depend on the attitude of the local authority as to whether or not you will be permitted to form a playgroup, and what conditions they will lay down as to its methods of operation.

In some areas, candidates for the role of playgroup leader are required to undertake a short course of instruction provided by the local authority. Income from such a venture as this is likely to be modest but it could make a useful contribution to your family budget.

Publishing

In today's complex society, people in all walks of life need information. Some need specialist information to carry out their jobs or to run their businesses; others need it to pursue their leisure interests. The entire newspaper, magazine and trade press is based on this thirst for information and much of the content of radio and television programmes is devoted to satisfying this demand. Economic considerations, however, preclude the majority of these organs from conveying information that is of interest only to minority groups. This leaves a wide field of opportunity for what is known as newsletter publishing.

Revenue comes from subscriptions and the sale of advertising space. As with all business ventures, one starts by discovering a need for a specialised service by a narrow sector of the population and finding out whether or not this is currently being met. The sector for your initial venture could be very modest: a newsletter addressed specifically to retired people, for example, containing information about local facilities. This could include details of shops and restaurants with street-level entrances; lifts between floors; seating for customers waiting to be served; local businesses offering discounts to pensioners over a range of products and services, as well as a list of forthcoming local events likely to interest the older generation.

You will need to have the use of a typewriter and a duplicator or photocopier. Most local associations of one kind or another possess duplicating equipment which is used only occasionally to run off announcements for circulation to members. A relatively modest donation to their funds might well secure for you the use of a machine during the time they are not requiring it themselves.

You can, of course, set your sights higher than the local scene, producing newsletters for distribution to special-interest groups throughout your region or, indeed, nationwide. Since it is the quality of the information provided, rather than the appearance of the publication, that will be important to your readers, presentation can be reasonably cheap and cheerful. Success will result from your ability to obtain regular items of information relevant to the needs of your readership and to identify and locate those for whom it will be important.

Repairing

The repair market extends from cars to bone china, musical instruments to boats and bicycles. Unless you have training and experience behind you, setting yourself up as a professional repairer could be hazardous. Through ineptitude, you could cause further damage to customers' property entrusted to your care. A further barrier to the adoption of this form of self-employment is likely to be the cost of acquiring the necessary tools and equipment.

There are, of course, certain types of repair work where the outlay on equipment will be relatively small, such as bicycle or tailoring repairs. These and similar low set-up cost repair activities may be within your reach and, subject to your possession of suitable skills, could be developed into profitable business ventures. They can be run from home because, if the service you provide is not easily come by in your locality, customers will find you. But take out some form of liability insurance to cover you should you be faced with a claim for negligence.

Teaching and tutoring

If you are a former school teacher and are familiar with the current syllabus for school examinations, you can undertake private coaching. If mathematics or science is your special subject, you should have little difficulty in obtaining pupils. In addition, you can apply to your local education authority to be put on their books for supply teaching.

But the teaching market does not stop here. If you have a teaching diploma in music or in speech and drama, dancing or foreign languages, you can set yourself up as a tutor in such subjects. The teaching of English to foreigners, particularly overseas business people, provides another opportunity.

There is also scope for self-employment by giving instruction in non-academic subjects. If sufficiently skilled and knowledgeable, you can run art classes, teach flower arranging or all manner of craftwork. The demand for such services is growing with the increasing interest in leisure pursuits generally.

Telephone message-taking

Here is a service that can be undertaken as a sideline by anyone working for themselves at home. Many small businesses are run by individuals whose activities take them away from their homes or offices during working hours. They have no one to deal with telephone messages, enquiries or orders in their absence. The telephone answering machine does not meet this need. Very often, callers prefer to speak to a person, not a machine: they ring off and contact an alternative supplier of the goods or services they require. The advantage of the human message-taker, is that the caller knows that the message has been received and understood and has greater confidence that required action will be taken. Furthermore, the message-taker can be briefed by his or her client to ask any pertinent questions of the caller, to clarify the content of the message and the action required.

Fees for rendering this service can be based on the number of messages taken and passed on. Depending on the number of calls you wish to handle per day, you could take on several clients, providing their particular business interests and activities do not conflict.

Tele-sales servicing

The distribution of goods from manufacturers or wholesalers to their business customers – retail shops, restaurants, hotels, factories – requires efficient administration in order to be cost-effective. Companies need to know the requirements of their customers in sufficient time for orders to be collated and vehicles loaded and despatched in accordance with pre-arranged schedules. To assist this process, many large firms employ teams of tele-sales operators, whose task it is to telephone customers at set times on particular days of the week or month, to ask for their orders. Their title is something of a misnomer, for little selling, in the usual sense, is actually involved. Their call is a reminder to the customer to check stock and tell them what he wants and in what quantity so that the order can be transmitted immediately to the dispatchers.

The same need applies equally to smaller producers and distributors. However, the cost involved in the permanent employment of tele-sales personnel is, for them, often prohibitive. The work can be farmed out to reliable home-based freelancers. A tele-sales agency, serving the needs of a group of non-competing producers is a viable proposition if you have a good telephone manner and some understanding of business practice. You will, of course, need a telephone and a fax machine would also be useful. It would enable you to transmit customers' detailed orders faster and more cheaply than by means of dictation over the telephone.

Translating

The potential demand for translation services has never been greater. The arrival of the Single European Market, coupled with ever-increasing world trade, provides an excellent opportunity to develop a profitable translation business. The essential requirement is a reading knowledge of at least one foreign language. Ideally, one should also have some commercial or technical knowledge. This is because much of the work will involve the translation of technical manuals or advertising brochures as well as trade correspondence.

If you have contacts who are fully conversant with a language different from your own speciality and they are prepared to collaborate with you, it will broaden the scope of your agency. You will need a typewriter or, better still, a word-processor. This is an activity where you do not need to restrict the geographical limits of your market. If you can obtain the occasional use of someone else's fax machine and can quote their number, you can put yourself in immediate touch with potential clients located in London and other major business centres.

Your fee rates are likely to be considerably lower than those of translation agencies based in high rental areas. Many firms seeking translation services put their work to established agencies and you may be able to obtain a share of this on a sub-contract basis. You should also make a point of letting your local Chamber of Commerce and local Enterprise Agency know of your existence. They are likely to receive enquiries from firms and individuals seeking translation services.

Supply and demand will dictate the level of fees you can command. Because the majority of translators offer French and German, the rates for these languages are low compared to those for Japanese, Chinese, Arabic and Russian, for which translation services are in great demand.

Typing and secretarial

A skilled typist, with the use of a good quality electronic typewriter, should be able to earn more working freelance at home for several clients than the salary received by the majority of permanently employed secretaries. But the problem is to find a regular volume of work. Home typists normally find work among small firms, doctors, clergymen, architects and local associations, whose work-load is insufficient to warrant the employment of a full-time secretary.

One of the drawbacks to freelance typing is the amount of time that can be taken up collecting and delivering work, as well as the variable legibility of copy that can slow typing output. This problem is reduced if you are able to do audio-typing. It cuts out the time involved in taking dictation in shorthand or having to decipher poor handwriting.

A means of adding to your income is to offer your services to firms that regularly mail circulars to customers. The work usually is straightforward, consisting of typing envelopes (or labels) with individual names and addresses, putting circulars into the envelopes and posting them. In practice, you should organise the entire operation from home, using outworkers to type and fill the envelopes.

A point to consider is that you should take out liability insurance if you have clients who frequently visit your home to bring or collect work. If a client breaks a leg because your front path is iced over and he slips, you could face a damages claim.

2.2 OPTIONS INVOLVING MODERATE TRAVELLING

We now come to the second group of activities, which will mainly be conducted on customers' premises.

Bookkeeping

There are thousands of small businesses being run by principals whose understanding of accounting procedures often is only rudimentary and, in some cases, non-existent. If you have some work experience in bookkeeping and know how to account for VAT, you could set up a freelance bookkeeping service, keeping the books of small local firms. If your knowledge and experience extends to computer skills, your services will be in even greater demand and should be reflected in your fees. These should be based on an hourly rate. You will need to make regular visits to clients' premises, spending a few hours weekly at each of them, to maintain their records efficiently.

One of the major problems besetting most small firms is control of the cash flow. The inflow of receipts from debtors does not synchronise with the need to pay creditors on time. This can result in the stoppage of essential supplies; production may be dislocated and the goodwill of customers placed in jeopardy. Similarly, the failure of many small business owners to keep proper accounts lands them in very serious difficulties with Customs and Excise inspectors, due to errors made in their VAT returns. A freelance bookkeeper, who can exercise a polite yet firm discipline with his or her clients, often can make an invaluable contribution to the survival, let alone the success, of a small firm.

Business training

Among those forced into redundancy by the economic recession, there are many people with considerable business experience and expertise. These are assets that can be put to good use in the training of others. Over the last decade or so, business training agencies have mushroomed and now constitute a lucrative industry. Their services do not come cheaply, however, and many small firms cannot afford to use them. Yet their need for staff training is no less than that of large corporate organisations.

Being a proficient practitioner does not necessarily make you an equally good teacher. But if you have had experience as a manager or supervisor, responsible for instructing subordinates, you may be able to set up a business training agency, specialising in the particular activity with which you are most familiar.

You could arrange seminars in clients' premises to instruct their sales representatives, their tele-sales personnel or their middle or senior management.

Modern business training relies heavily on the use of theatre to instil facts and ideas. As well as subject knowledge, one needs to be able to project one's personality to perform successfully in this type of work. Your fee rates will have to take account of what your market will bear. But as a freelance operator with low overheads, you should be able to undercut the rates of larger agencies.

In addition to undertaking assignments with individual client companies, you could hold open seminars by hiring a public hall or room as a venue and canvassing local firms to enrol members of their staff as delegates. Free promotion of your services can often be achieved by joining a speakers' panel and addressing business association luncheons or dinners on a low- or no-fee basis, in order to gain the attention of potential clients among the audience.

Catering for functions

If you are a skilled and resourceful cook, launching an outside catering service could prove a lucrative venture. There is a regular market: birthday parties; private dinner parties; business lunches. You will need to be suitably equipped, with adequate oven, refrigerator and freezer capacity, space in which to prepare and collate meals, and transport you can rely on. Although you do not need formal qualifications, you should familiarise yourself with the legislation governing environmental health and the statutory hygiene regulations. These are obtainable from HMSO. Before preparing food at home for sale, you should inform your local environmental health inspector and your local planning officer. Furthermore, you should take out public liability insurance as a safeguard should anyone suffer food poisoning as the result of eating a meal you have provided.

Prepare balanced menus consisting of your most successful dishes but be prepared to vary them to take account of individual customer preferences. More and more people are becoming diet conscious and you should certainly include vegetarian dishes in your selection.

You will need to establish with your customer who will supply cutlery and crockery, whether facilities exist at the venue for keeping hot dishes hot and cold dishes cold and for washing up crockery and cutlery afterwards. Charges should be per head and take account of whether you or your customer will serve the meal. Catering is labour-intensive, involving shopping, food preparation, cooking, serving and subsequent clearing up. Depending on the number of meals to be conveyed to the venue and served, you may need extra pairs of hands to help you. This will increase your costs and must be reflected in your charges.

Imagination in the composition of dishes and their presentation, combined with method in the way in which the work is organised, is essential for success in this business. One should also have in mind, however, the natural anxiety of clients when engaging an outside catering service that all will go well. It is important that you, and any staff you have to assist you, should exhibit a degree of professionalism coupled with a pleasant and helpful manner towards the hosts and their guests. In this way, you will secure the all-important personal recommendations that will bring you further bookings.

Curtain and loose cover making

The skills needed for making-up curtains and loose covers are often self-taught. If you are adept at needlework and have or can acquire some experience in measuring for loose covers, there is an available market you can enter. Profits will depend largely on your productivity, and a suitable powered sewing machine will be essential. Beyond that, start-up costs could be minimal.

You can offer your services either direct to the public or to those shops and stores in your locality selling soft furnishing materials that provide a making-up service to their clientele. You will need transport in order to visit clients' homes to take measurements and deliver completed goods. Shops and stores will normally tell you the rate of payment they are willing to offer for your work. So far as the work you do for individual householders is concerned, you will have to decide your own pricing structure but a little research among local stores should give you the guidance you need. There are many books on loose cover and curtain making that should be available to you from your public library.

Decorating

Despite the large numbers of able-bodied householders who carry out their own interior and exterior decorating, there remains a considerable market for the professional. If you have acquired skills and experience in house painting and decorating and are physically able to carry out this sort of work on a regular basis, you can earn a living. Your market will include the more well-heeled homeowners in your locality, as well as women living on their own and elderly people unable to undertake such work themselves. In addition, there is likely to be a sprinkling of younger people who have never wielded a paintbrush and have no intention of ever doing so!

Promote your business by dropping leaflets through letter boxes and putting cards in newsagents' windows. But personal recommendation should provide your main source of extra business. Remember that it is often the little things that count in this kind of service business: a cheerful yet respectful attitude; minimising the disturbance caused to clients while the work is in progress; clearing up and cleaning up at the end of each day's work.

You should be able to negotiate a commission with your builders' merchant when you buy materials on behalf of your clients. Where a job requires any considerable outlay by you for paint and wallpaper, obtain an interim payment on account from your customer. You will need transport to convey yourself and your equipment to clients' homes. Ladders, trestles and other necessary equipment can be hired on a daily or weekly basis from locally based tool-hire firms, until such time as you are in a position to finance their purchase.

Dog exercising

Every dog should be taken for at least one regular walk each day. Larger breeds may need to be exercised off the lead in some suitable open space. In households where all the adult members are working full-time this poses obvious problems. If you can handle dogs responsibly, you can earn money by providing a dog exercising service for such people, as well as for the elderly and the house-bound.

Possession of a vehicle to travel from one client's home to another could be a time-saving advantage and will be necessary if you need to transport dogs to and from distant parks or other open spaces. Since you will be responsible for the animals in your care, it may be prudent to take out liability insurance cover, should any dog cause, or incur, injury.

Domestic cleaning service

With the comparatively large number of women now pursuing careers, the problem of obtaining and retaining reliable domestic help is a very real one. The advantage of using the service of an agency, rather than employing cleaners themselves, is the greater assurance they have that the work will get done when it is required to be done.

In setting up a domestic cleaning agency you do not need any formal qualifications. But you do need to be an organised individual and be able to organise others. There may be occasions when, rather than let a client down, you will have to tackle the work yourself if a cleaner suddenly is unavailable.

You will need to recruit a reliable team of workers and have the means of transporting them. In a period of high unemployment, recruitment should not prove too difficult. Young people, especially students, who are adaptable and are eager for the chance to earn extra money, should be easy to recruit, especially if you offer payment above the going rate. By setting them to work in pairs, the cleaning of each home should be completed within two to three hours on average, if it is being done on a regular basis.

It is essential in this type of activity to maintain proper records, both of staff payments and for the regular invoicing of clients. Slow-paying customers can be a problem. You will need to take a firm line to avoid debtors falling into arrears. This is a lucrative but highly competitive market and your level of service will need to match or surpass that of the competition. A reputation for reliability will prove to be your greatest asset.

Driving

Providing you have a well-maintained car and a clean driving licence, you could obtain driving work through local car hire firms. Although these generally supply cars with drivers on demand, many do use the services of freelance drivers using their own vehicles. You will be required to take out special insurance and this will have to be taken into account, together with the cost of petrol and of vehicle depreciation, when considering the available rates of payment for your services.

These will depend on the locality and the size and standing of the cab firm, whose management will decide the rates charged to passengers, based on mileage and the time of day or night at which the journey takes place. The usual procedure is for the driver to collect fares, passing a percentage on to the hire firm for introducing the business.

An alternative method is for the hire firm to agree a flat rate charge with the freelance drivers on its list, which is payable on a weekly basis. A major drawback for many people is the need to work long hours in the evening and often well into the night, in order to secure a reasonable income.

Executive 'temping'

The uncertain trading conditions of recent years have had a dramatic effect on the way many companies are recruiting their executives. Increasing numbers of firms show a disinclination to tie themselves to long-term employment agreements at boardroom level. The costs associated with employing executives – sickness benefit, pensions, provision of an office and a secretary, holidays, company-owned cars and employer's national insurance contributions – can be as much again as an individual's annual salary. As a result, engaging the services of a temporary executive for a fee-rate varying from £200 to £500 per day, is proving a more advantageous arrangement.

Seniors managers, displaced by the recession, often find executive 'temping' attractive. It offers a means of reviving their careers at a time when corporate re-employment can be very difficult to achieve.

If you have the requisite trouble-shooting skills and experience, you can register with a career management agency specialising in interim management. Operating as a self-employed practitioner, you should be able to build up a network of clients and achieve an income at least equal to that which you would earn on a permanently employed basis and probably considerably higher. Many such independent executives aim to work for client firms for a minimum of 10–14 days each month, devoting the remainder of their time to marketing their practices and preparing for future work.

Floral display service

Floral displays provide an attractive decorative feature in the public rooms of hotels, restaurants and conference centres, as well as the reception areas of business offices. With a knowledge of flower arranging plus an understanding of the care of indoor plants and shrubs, you could consider setting up a floral display services agency.

You will need transport to collect and deliver between florists, garden centres and your clients' premises. It is a business you can conduct from your own home, providing you have space in which to prepare displays. Maintenance and the regular substitution of displays will be a routine task. As with all service operations, good organisation is essential.

Take appropriate examples of your work along to prospective clients so they can see for themselves what you have to offer and ask them to give you a contract for a trial period of, say, a month. This will enable them to judge the reliability of your service.

Gardening

Most people like to look at a well-kept garden; only a minority are keen to put in the effort to maintain it on a regular basis. Jobbing gardening, therefore, is an obvious activity to be considered, especially if you possess 'green fingers' and enjoy this kind of work.

Keen amateur gardeners generally prefer to do their own plant maintenance but have problems when on holiday. Many contract gardeners meet this need by offering a one-off garden care service. With charges in the region of £15 per hour, this means that customers taking holidays can have their gardens maintained for £30–45 per week in their absence. Depending on the distance to be travelled, you may also be able to charge a call-out fee.

The care of indoor plants poses another problem when owners are away. If you have a suitable greenhouse and some botanical knowledge, you could arrange either to water such plants in situ or to collect and maintain them until customers return. Charge rates should be varied to take account of the size and fragile nature of the plants involved.

Garden design

An interesting and financially rewarding activity for those with a flair for design, coupled with some botanical knowledge, is garden design. A journal called *Landscape Design* published by the Landscape Institute will be helpful, and the Institute of Horticulture should also be able to provide you with assistance. You should also ask the adult education department of your county council if courses on this subject are available locally.

A considerable amount of labouring will be involved in laying out clients' gardens, so you are likely to need physical help for the heavy work. Tools can be bought second-hand or hired. Negotiate with your local garden centre and a building materials supplier for a commission on plants and materials that you order on your clients' behalf. Arrangements should be made with clients to ensure that you receive either immediate reimbursement for such costs or an interim payment of part of your fee on account.

The most successful garden designers are those who can win the confidence of their clients at an early stage and guide them in the selection of the most suitable scheme to meet their individual needs. Much can be learned about garden design from books but you should also visit as many gardens as you can that are open to public viewing in order to study how the most pleasing aspects have been contrived.

Hairdressing

If you are a trained hairdresser, you could consider setting up a mobile hairdressing business, visiting customers in their own homes. The provision of this service has reached close to saturation point in some areas, and you will need to do a considerable amount of research to discover whether there is room for yet another contender in your locality. Start-up costs need not be high, providing you already possess your basic working equipment. You will need a car, a telephone and an answering machine on which to record bookings during your absence.

In tourist areas, there is a market among local hotels, attending to the hair of guests. You will need to pay a percentage of your fees to the hotels that permit you to work on their premises. Hairdressing is so personal a service that, apart from being a good hairdresser, you also need a pleasingly out-going personality that will ensure you are a welcome visitor in your clients' homes.

Home-sitting service

A problem that concerns many householders when taking a weekend break or an annual holiday of two or three weeks, is the care of pets, upkeep of the garden and leaving their home unattended. By using a specialist home-sitting service, their home is protected from thieves or squatters; dogs and cats are cared for in their familiar surroundings without the costs of kennel and cattery fees, while lawns get cut and garden plants watered.

The best way to start such a operation is to do the sitting yourself in the early days. You will find out at first hand the type of problems most likely to arise before engaging the services of freelance sitters, to expand the business.

You will need to adopt a very strict set of rules governing the performance of the sitters you engage. The length of time they may be away from the property must be limited. They should receive no visitors to the house unless the owners have given their specific consent. It would be advisable for you to make spot checks yourself at varying times to ensure that sitters are abiding by the rules you have stipulated.

Firms that operate such a service often apply a basic one-off setting-up fee in the region of £25, plus a daily fee of between £15 and £20, which covers looking after the client's home plus light maintenance work in the garden. Extra duties required of sitters, such as taking care of pets, attract a small extra charge. In addition, the client pays the sitter a sum in the region of £20–£25 per week for subsistence, together with petrol expenses to and from the property at an agreed rate per mile.

The fee paid to the sitter will vary between £25 and £30 per week, with increments to cover the care of pets or other additional duties. The viability of the business depends on being able to recruit sitters of the appropriate calibre. Retired couples who are responsible and dependable could be well suited to such work.

Market research interviewing

Most of us, at one time or another, have been approached in the street by an interviewer working for a market research firm and been invited to contribute to a survey by answering a series of questions relating to particular products or social issues. Rather fewer are the numbers of people interviewed in their own homes, where the scope and depth of the survey is likely to be more detailed.

Becoming a market research interviewer is a means of working for yourself and earning a reasonable income. You will have to put up with the occasional rigours of the British climate as well as the inevitable frustrations involved in dealing with the British public! But if you can handle these, you can earn in the region of £40–£50 per day plus expenses.

The major market research firms provide short training courses for interviewers and a list of such organisations can be obtained from the Market Research Society. Where the needs of a survey require interviews to be conducted in people's homes, it is often necessary to work in the evenings and at weekends. You will need to be a fairly unperturbed person with a persistent streak to your character. Research companies usually set precise requirements as to the type and number of respondents to be interviewed in order to achieve an appropriate balance of views. You will be spending your time talking to people and an outgoing personality is very necessary for success in this kind of work.

Office-cleaning agency

The contract cleaning of office premises has become a highly competitive business which, without considerable resources for promotion, a newcomer would find it difficult to enter in major city areas. On the other hand, there are many suburban and provincial centres and industrial estates, where firms are still victim to the idiosyncrasies of the traditional 'Mrs Mopps', not all of whom can be relied upon to put in a consistent appearance.

Unlike a domestic cleaning service, which can usually be undertaken during normal working hours, office cleaning must be done either early in the morning before clerical staff arrive or in the late evening, once they have left. This makes the recruitment of cleaning personnel more difficult, because the nature of the task involves anti-social hours.

You will need a vehicle in which to transport operatives from one job to the next, as well as equipment, such as industrial cleaners and floor-polishers. Office cleaning must be done on a daily basis, rather than the few times per week normally considered to be sufficient by the domestic householder. However, if you can acquire the equipment and bring together a small, reliable team of workers, you may find considerable scope for such a service among small offices located in your area.

Party-plan agency

Pioneered in this country by a manufacturer of plastic storage
containers, the party-plan method is now used to sell a wide
range of merchandise direct to consumers. The basis of the plan
is the appointment of locally-based agents by the promoter. The
agents' principal task is to recruit numbers of householders willing to host tea or coffee parties in their own homes. Guests,
drawn from among neighbours and friends, are served light
refreshments at the host's expense, while the agent displays sam-
ples of the products supplied by the promoting manufacturer.
The agent takes orders for these goods, which are subsequently
delivered to the host, whose responsibility it is to distribute them
to the customers concerned. Payment is obtained either at the
time the order is placed or upon delivery. The host receives a
gift in kind from the promoter – usually an item from the product range – as compensation for holding the party. The agent
receives a commission based on the value of the orders
obtained.

Goods that are sold by this method include fashion-wear, baby-
wear and housewares of all kinds. Such 'lines' usually are not
available through retail shops, and the producer, by retaining
the shopkeepers' mark-up, is in a position to offer the agent a
comparatively high rate of commission. Apart from actually selling the goods, which is unlikely to be particularly onerous in the
relaxed atmosphere created by the venue, the agent's main concern is to recruit a sufficient number of hosts to provide regular
gatherings of potential customers.

In order to become a party-plan agent, you can either apply to
an organisation already promoting this form of marketing or
approach manufacturers with a proposal to set up such a
scheme on their behalf in your locality. The work can be lucrative providing you have a sufficiently wide circle of friends and
acquaintances you can persuade to host such parties.

Pet-minding

Care for pets, such as cats, caged birds and tropical fish, always
presents problems for their owners when away from home for
holiday or business reasons. A mobile pet-minding service pro-

vides a welcome solution. Provided you have transport, you could set up an agency, basing your charges on the period of time you spend visiting each client's home. Find your initial clientele in the area close to where you live. Not only will this reduce your travelling time and costs: it is likely to reduce your clients' possible anxiety about entrusting you with the keys to their homes. Obviously, you should be prepared to supply references when required. But as a local person, whose integrity can be vouched for by neighbours and other local acquaintances you are likely to be more readily accepted than a stranger from another district.

You will need to keep a careful record of time spent at each home and to call and collect the payment due soon after your clients return. In this way, you will avoid the cost of sending out invoices and reduce the danger of bad debts.

Snack lunch service

Supplying ready-made sandwiches, crisps, biscuits and soft drinks to the staff of small and medium-sized commercial and industrial firms where there is no staff canteen provided, can be a profitable venture.

You must comply with the environmental health regulations, which means talking to your local inspector in advance to starting to trade. As with all catering activities, the work is highly labour-intensive. It will also involve working anti-social hours. Freshly-made sandwiches must be prepared in the morning of the day on which they are sold.

The market for lunchtime snacks usually is very accessible and convenient, because the majority of offices are situated in blocks and small factories are concentrated in industrial estates. The convenience of having snacks delivered rather than having to send out to shops, located in busy town-centre areas where parking is difficult, has created a demand for this service.

Success lies in making deliveries to firms at the same time each day and offering a selection of sandwiches with attractive fillings, hygienically wrapped and pleasantly presented. It is a cash business – you get paid on delivery – and start-up costs are likely to be minimal. You need transport, however. You can operate from home providing that you have adequate space to prepare your wares under hygienic conditions.

2.3 OPTIONS INVOLVING CONSIDERABLE TRAVELLING

For this third group of activities, you will need to be highly mobile and the use of a car will be essential.

Antiques dealing

Some people acquire, over a period of time, a considerable collection of objects which are of antique interest. If you are such an individual and are prepared to subdue any sentimental attachment you may have formed for such bric-à-brac, you could consider a business in antique dealing, using your personal possessions as your initial stock-in-trade.

The hire of a stall in a market is unlikely to overstrain your pocket, though you do need to choose a good location. Some towns have bric-à-brac markets on different days of the week to their general markets. You should spend some time researching those within reasonable travelling distance of your home. Keep in mind the fact that the level of trading in certain towns or districts is considerably more up-market than in others. Practised dealers in antiques often buy items in cheaper markets for subsequent resale in areas where the prices they will fetch will be higher.

You will, therefore, need to visit antique markets regularly, in order to keep yourself informed as to what other dealers currently are buying and the prices at which various items are being purchased and sold. There are fashions in the world of antiques collecting and you will need to know what is in vogue. Read up as much as you can about the subject generally by using your public library and talking to established dealers.

Eventually, you can extend the scope of your operations by undertaking house clearance, the source from which the bulk of antiques originate. Before doing so, however, you will need a storage area and to have an arrangement with one or more general second-hand dealers in order to dispose of the non-antique items included in the clearances.

Business consultancy

Many redundant executives, possessing specific experience and expertise, set themselves up as consultants to business firms. Initially they tend to undertake assignments with their previous employers and former business contacts, using referrals from these ultimately to extend their client-base. To be a successful freelance trouble-shooter, one must possess diagnostic skills, a thorough grasp of one's specialised subject and the ability to work, in an authoritative yet pleasant manner, with people at all levels within client firms.

Independent consultants generally secure fees for their services of between £300 and £500 per day, as against large, multi-partner practices that will normally charge at least twice as much. However, in a one-man or one-woman practice, consultants must spend a considerable proportion of their time negotiating for assignments. Their utilisation rate – the proportion of their total working hours that is actually spent on assignments and for which they are paid – may not be much above fifty per cent.

Providing one has a car and telephone, start-up costs can be modest. In order to extend your client-base beyond that of your existing contacts, however, the provision of a well-designed brochure that sets out your specific skills and experience is considered essential.

Consultancy covers a wide spectrum of activities from management and marketing to the provision of advice on such diverse subjects as energy conservation, recycling of waste materials, factory layout and plant installation, staff recruitment and training, advertising and publicity, and finance. There is hardly an aspect of commerce or industry that does not provide the opportunity for freelance consultancy services. If you have thoughts along these lines, there is plenty of scope but you must possess recognisable expertise in your chosen speciality.

Buying agency

Those who possess in-depth experience in procurement, either within the public or the private sector, could consider setting up as buying agents. Within many trades and industries there are firms frequently in need of new sources of supply for existing products or supply sources for new products. Buying agents normally work for several non-competing client firms. They receive an agreed rate of commission based on either the volume or the monetary value of the goods they source.

Obviously, one has need of knowledge of the markets in which one intends to operate, as well as good negotiating skills. The work may entail considerable travel at home and abroad and linguistic skills will be advantageous. Narrow specialisation in products and markets is advisable in order to maintain an expert knowledge in the face of technological and commercial change. Travel and communication costs are likely to be high but much of these may be recoverable from clients, particularly where the work results from specific assignments.

Craftwork

There is a considerable market for craftwork of all kinds, but the only way you can reach it is by taking a stall at a craft fair. These are held in venues all over the country. Those located in tourist areas usually are the most effective but the rental charges for the stalls is proportionately higher. Spend time visiting as many fairs as you can. Take note of the number of actual sales being made. Craft fairs usually attract crowds of people, especially on wet Sunday afternoons when there is nowhere else to go! Visitors are out of the rain and there is plenty for them to see. The question you must ask yourself is how many of them are really interested in craftwork and are prepared to spend their money buying it.

Not only will your choice of venue be important: so will the position of your stall within the hall or marquee. Stalls do not come cheaply: anything from £20 to £50 per day, depending on the venue. This will involve investing some of your limited cash up front, in what is, for the uninitiated, a considerable speculation. However, apart from the items you may be able to sell on the day, there is always a good possibility that you will receive enquiries from customers potentially interested in your work that could result in useful subsequent commissions.

The range of craft activity is wide: artificial flower-making; artificial jewellery-making; candle-making; carpentry and joinery;

egg decoration; enamelling; leatherwork; pottery; rug and car-pet-making; tapestry-work and toy-making, to name but a few.

You will need a car or a van to transport your wares, as well as a spare room, garage or other outbuilding in which to carry out the work. Use of any part of your home to produce goods for profit will require you to conform to local authority regulations that control such activities. *The Craftsman Magazine,* a bi-monthly publication, contains much advice and items of news regarding crafts and those who perform them. It also provides details of forthcoming craft fairs.

Family history research

In districts where the population consists of a sufficient number of people with the disposable income to satisfy their curiosity, setting up an ancestry research service can be a profitable ven-ture. Obviously, you will need to know or to find out how such research is carried out. Use your public library to read up on the subject. The Society of Genealogists can also be very helpful to you in this respect. Its library contains copies of parish registers and family histories that provide a wealth of information.

Before launching your business, try to trace your own ancestry or that of one of your friends. It will highlight some of the prob-lems and the means to overcome them. The experience will also give you a degree of confidence that will help you to sell your service to potential clients. Your main expenditure will be for travel, postage, and copies of birth and marriage certificates. This will be recoverable from clients in addition to your research fees. Your research time, including travelling time if you have to cover any considerable distances to obtain information, should be charged on an hourly basis.

It is important that clients should understand that results can-not be guaranteed. All you can offer is your research time and they will be expected to pay for this, whatever the final outcome. If essential records do not exist they cannot be traced and the research will be abortive. Before starting any work on a project, a written contract that stipulates this condition should be entered into with the client. Initially, you should seek prepayment of part of your fees. This will finance your travel and other out-of-pocket expenses.

To avoid the cost of advertising, make direct approach to people who are prominent in your local area and whom you judge could afford the service. Do this by means of an introductory letter, followed by a personal visit to discuss the service in detail. Subsequent promotion of your business should be sought by means of press releases to local newspapers and the offer of talks to Rotary or Lions Clubs and similar organisations in the area. There is wide public interest in the subject of ancestry research and you should seek every opportunity to gain free publicity for your service.

Hospitality broking

Corporate hospitality, whereby business firms entertain groups of their most important customer contacts at major sporting events, such as Cheltenham Races on Gold Cup day, Wimbledon Fortnight, Open golf tournaments or Formula 3 training on a grand prix circuit, are considered good for business. Host companies are prepared to spend considerable sums of money to gain the undivided attention of their vital contacts for an entire day.

Hospitality broking provides a service to such firms seeking suitable venues for corporate entertaining. Brokers save client companies the time and the trouble involved in obtaining details and prices for such events. The firms concerned do not pay for this service because the broker receives a commission from the organisers of the event when the party booking is made.

If you decide to become a hospitality broker, you will need to target a selected sector of the market, preferably locally-based small firms, whom the larger brokers do not bother with. On the supply side, look for reasonably modest events and venues, where costs will not be exorbitant: local festivals and shows, concerts, visits to stately homes. Brief the personnel of the client company to ensure that their guests get the fullest enjoyment out of the day. The chosen venue should be convenient for their contacts and invitations should be sent out early to achieve a maximum attendance. The object will be to provide guests with a day they will long remember. Programmes and menus should bear the logo of the host company together with the date, to provide a souvenir of the occasion. Suitable gifts for both men and women in the party should be presented to them on departure.

To operate a hospitality broking service you will need to negotiate satisfactory commission arrangements with the organisers of suitable events and functions as well as introducing yourself to appropriate companies in your local area who are likely to be interested in customer hospitality. You will need an outgoing personality plus good organising ability. Start-up costs can be modest. Apart from a car, you will need a telephone and fax machine (which can be rented) and, ideally, a well-designed brochure that describes your service.

Interpreting

Fluency in at least two foreign languages is not the only qualification one needs to earn a living as an interpreter. The very nature of the work – assisting two or more people to converse over what could be a wide range of subjects – demands quick thinking and a background understanding of business and related subjects, as well as considerable resilience. Travelling to exhibitions, conferences and business meetings will be time-consuming and could involve working unsocial hours.

Interpreters also find work as couriers for travel agents and as guides for such organisations as the English Tourist Authority. Fees vary widely according to the scarcity-value of interpreters in different tongues. Japanese and Chinese rate highest, followed closely by Arabic and Russian. Lower rates apply for Western European languages.

Lecturing and public speaking

If you have some experience of addressing groups of people and can do so in a fluent and interesting manner, you have the capability to earn money from lecturing and public speaking. Good speakers are always in demand. Opportunities to address social organisations, such as Women's Institutes, Rotary and Lions Clubs and luncheon clubs, as well as business conferences and seminars, are widely available. A lot of travelling is likely but this expense is often recoverable from the event organisers.

Fees will vary according to the size of the audience and the prestige of the occasion. The more experienced the speaker, the higher become the fees he or she can command.

To break into this field, you will need to acquire a fund of knowledge on, perhaps, three specific subjects on which your talks can be based. You can read up the techniques of speech preparation and delivery in a number of books that have been published on the subject in recent years. Invite bookings by approaching organisations that you know engage speakers to address meetings, luncheons or dinners. Find out the name of the individual responsible for organising such occasions and write saying that you have a number of prepared talks that you believe could be of interest to members. If you have subjects that are appropriate, you could also offer your services as a lecturer for professional courses run by Colleges of Further Education.

Essentially, you should find out as much as you can about the likely composition and the expectations of the audience in advance. Ensure that what you have to say is geared to their particular needs and interests. Always have a discernible theme, learn how to project both your voice and your personality and leave your audience with something to think about once you have sat down. A practised speaker can make a talk on even the most mundane or hackneyed subject memorable for his audience by finding a new slant. Topicality, too, often can introduce a new element to an old theme.

The field of opportunity is wide and the number of people capable of interesting and entertaining an audience is relatively few. Even if your current public speaking experience is limited, bear in mind that this is an art that is acquired, not a natural gift. Practice and perseverance will make a more than passable speaker out of any reasonably intelligent individual.

Sales agency

If you have a background in selling and now find yourself out of work due to company cut-back or failure, you could consider setting up as a freelance sales agent. The fundamentals of successful selling are the ability to discover needs on the part of potential customers and to satisfy them by the supply of suitable goods or services.

It would be advisable to keep to a product or service area or an industry familiar to you and where you have some existing contacts. Using both supplier and customer contacts and working on commission based on selling prices, you could build an income with a range of product lines. Ensure that the interests of suppliers do not overlap, provide a high personal sales service to your customers and adopt efficient working methods. You will need a car – preferably with a car telephone, so that you can reach, and be reached by – your customers while you are travelling. If funds allow, you should also consider acquiring an answering machine and a fax, so that messages can be received at home during your absence.

One of the advantages that the freelance salesperson has over company representatives, is that a far wider range of goods or services can be offered to customers from a variety of suppliers. This factor should enable you to reach your income targets working within a reasonably limited geographical area. In this way, you can reduce the travelling time between calls and make considerable savings in terms of petrol usage and car depreciation.

Endeavour to tie in with supplier firms not already represented in your area. With the advent of the Single European Market, the scope for a freelance sales agency is considerably extended. Many of the smaller European producers seek to enter the United Kingdom market and look for local representation. Consider joining the British Agents Register. They receive many enquiries from both home-based and foreign firms looking for representation. They also possess a computerised system that links the needs of principals to the specific qualifications and territories of their subscribing agents.

The above list represents a mere selection of possible options. It has been devised to illustrate the wide variety of business opportunities that are available to those without capital. It is by no means exhaustive and one constantly learns of individuals with imagination and flair who have discovered new ways of setting themselves up in business on what is often no more than a shoestring. None of the listed options is dependent on the availability of a capital sum; but whatever you decide to do, obviously some out-of-pocket expenditure will be involved. In a later chapter we shall look at ways to keep your business expenditure to a minimum. Meanwhile, if you have a residue of redundancy money or a small sum set aside in a savings account, this should be sufficient to meet initial expenditures. If all else fails, most homes harbour some no longer used items that could fetch ready cash if sold to a second-hand dealer.

Some of the listed options may not appear to offer a sufficient level of income by themselves, but there are instances where two or three activities can be grouped. Family History Research and House Research are obvious examples. So, too, is the bracketing of Home-Sitting and Pet-Minding, to which Dog Exercising is an obvious addition.

A careful study of the list of options should spark trains of thought in your mind that will suggest other opportunities. These may relate to your own particular experience and abilities or to needs that are apparent to you in your local area.

2.4 TESTING OPTIONS FOR VIABILITY

Whether you decide to adopt one of the options that have been listed or to pursue an opportunity of your own devising, as a first step you should test its viability. This is best achieved by posing a number of questions, on the following lines:

- Who will use this service?
- Why will they use it?
- How many will use it?
- How much and how often will they use it?
- What will they be prepared to pay for it?
- What will they expect the service to provide?
- How well do competitors currently provide this service?
- What scope is there to introduce improvements to the service that competitors currently provide?
- Why should this service continue to be needed in the future?
- What future events might curtail demand for this service?

- Do you have sufficient knowledge, experience or skills to provide this service?
- Do you have sufficient facilities (premises, equipment, transport) to provide this service?
- How promptly are you likely to get paid for providing this service?
- What expenditure are you likely to incur in setting up this service?
- Do you need any permits to supply this service?
- Will the level of profits you expect to receive from this service be sufficient to meet the income needs of yourself and your dependants?
- If you envisage conducting a number of activities, what percentage of your time is likely to be taken up in providing this service?
- To what extent will the provision of this service conflict with or be complementary to other activities you intend to pursue?
- What potential for future growth do you foresee for this service?

These questions will raise a host of other queries. In the following chapters we shall look at ways in which they can be answered.

3 Controlling the Money

3.1 WHY SMALL BUSINESSES FAIL

Small businesses have a high mortality rate. Most of those that fail do so within two to three years of being set up. Various reasons are advanced to explain why this occurs and there appear to be three principal causes of failure:

1. The market in which the firm hopes to operate has been insufficiently researched. The numbers of potential customers and their need for the product or service on offer is not as predicted. As a result, the volume of orders, or offers of work, is insufficient to provide the necessary inflow of revenue to sustain the business.
2. The business is under-funded. The capital sum available is insufficient to set the business up in a way that is appropriate to the kind of operation it is engaged in. Premises, or stocks, or production equipment are too limited and the business cannot perform adequately. Where the funding is too restricted, there is not enough money to support the operation during the initial period, when sales are relatively small and the revenue they generate does not cover costs.
3. The money side of the business is not managed properly. The majority of individuals who set up in business working for themselves usually have some experience either in selling or producing. Those who start a service business often do so because they have a particular skill or talent related to the work involved. Only a comparative few have an understanding of the financial difficulties involved in running a small business.

The need for a thorough research of your potential market has already been stressed and we shall look at ways of assessing the potential demand for your service in a later chapter. Meanwhile, we must consider this question of funding and, what is vitally important, how the money side of your business should be controlled.

Most businesses are set up with the investment of a capital sum. The funding is often drawn from two sources. Part of the capital is drawn from the personal resources of the proprietors, or the partners in a partnership, or the shareholders in the case of a private limited company. The other part is raised by means of a loan from a bank or some other lending institution. This is the normal method by which a business venture is financed. Without doubt, it is the best way to launch an enterprise, provided the total sum that is raised is adequate to cover the initial needs of the business during its first few months of operation. But as we noted in the opening chapter of this book, it is not an option available to all.

Setting up a business and making a success of the venture is always difficult. Setting up without capital is even more formidable. But we know it can be done because it has been done, many times, and, even in today's uncertain economic circumstances, it is still being done. No one could sensibly urge you to attempt it from choice. But if you have no choice and are determined to fend for yourself because you are convinced no one else will fend for you, then you can be successful.

There is, in fact, some virtue to be found in setting up without reliance on borrowed money. The absence of capital imposes a severe discipline at the inception of the business. We have already seen this at work in the restricted choice of operation you can effectively undertake. Without a capital sum at your disposal, you will be forced to be extremely economical in the way you launch your business. Whatever you provide for the business will, inevitably, be basic. There will be no extravagance, no unnecessary frills, because the money will not be available. This removes from your path the pitfall that unfortunately has trapped so many unwary proprietors of small firms, namely, the ill-considered use of the capital sum they have borrowed. So many inexperienced people have gone into business with a bank loan that has been frittered away on over-lavish office suites, impressive-looking motor cars, expensively designed promotional literature and other paraphernalia, all of which was intended, presumably, to create an image that would claim attention.

It is all too easy to fall into this trap. But the on-going burden of servicing the loan has to be carried in the months and the years that follow, contributing heavily to overheads that can become crippling once sales revenue begins to falter. Furthermore, in the event of a business that is dependent on borrowed money failing, the consequences for its owner can be dire. In the case of sole proprietorships and partnerships, the principals are personally liable for all debts incurred. Where the principals are shareholders and directors of a private limited company, their personal liability is limited so far as trading debts are concerned but, in most cases, they are liable to the bank for repayment of the start-up loan which they have personally guaranteed. But if you can succeed in setting up and sustaining your own business without borrowed money, you are truly independent. If the worst comes to the very worst and the business fails to provide you with an income, you are free to shut up shop and do something else, without any resulting penalty.

It is an option that hopefully you will not have to consider. Do your market research, know where you are going to find your future customers, calculate the approximate volume of work they are likely to offer you, be sure that you have the ability to satisfy their needs and you have the right ingredients for starting in business. Whether the business can be sustained, however, depends on how well you control the money side. This is what we are going to deal with in this chapter.

3.2 CALCULATING COSTS

The first thing you have to be sure about is that the business will be able to make ends meet: in other words, that it will earn enough money to cover its costs and make a profit. You may think that this is stating what is simply obvious. It may be obvious but it is not necessarily simple. Let us suppose that you set up as a contract gardener. You know about gardening. You already have gardening tools and items of equipment such as a hedge-trimmer and a lawn-mower and you have decided that you will cart them around in the boot of your car that you have already paid for. On the face of it, your overheads are going to be non-existent. Every time a customer pays you, you can put the money into your pocket and spend it as you like because it is pure profit.

Don't you believe it! You *will* have costs. Tools do not last for ever. If you use them every day, they will not last as long as you think, and will need replacement. Your equipment will need periodic servicing and so will your car. In fact, your car will need to be taxed, insured, maintained. One day, that, too, will have to be replaced. On top of all this, you will need to attract new customers. There is always movement in the market. People move into a house and want you to attend to their garden. They move out and a new owner arrives who prefers to do his own gardening. So you must constantly find new customers to replace those you lose. This means money has to be spent on advertising, even if it is only the cost of a card in a newsagent's window.

Depending on the size and scope of your service business, overhead costs will vary but, whatever the type of operation you decide to run, they will exist. The largest overhead cost of your business will be the cost of employing you. Making ends meet means generating enough revenue, in the form of customers' payments for your services, to cover all the costs incurred in running the business, including your own labour cost.

The costs of a business are of two kinds. There are certain expenditures, such as for labour, telephone rental, insurance and stationery, that have to be met regardless of the amount of activity the business is engaged in. For example, should you decide to take a week's holiday, you would earn no money during the seven days but you would still need to draw your salary, maintain your insurance cover and keep the telephone connected. During peak periods of the year, when your service could be in great demand, you could, perhaps, double your weekly earnings. But these sorts of cost would not double. They would remain constant. These constant costs are described in accountancy terms as the *fixed costs* of the business.

There are, however, other costs that the business will incur that are not constant. They will vary with the amount of work you undertake. These are petrol costs, bus and train fares, money spent on advertising. They are known as *variable costs*. By adding together the *fixed costs* and the *variable costs*, you have the *total costs* involved in operating the business. Initially, you will have to estimate your variable costs based on your anticipated level of activity. These cost calculations should be based on a specific period of time, such as a month, six months, or a year.

3.3   BREAKING EVEN

Until such time as your revenue (the amount of money coming into the business in the form of payments for the service you have provided) exceeds the amount of your total costs, you will not be making a profit. Providing the revenue does not dip below the amount of your total costs, the business will just survive. You will have nothing in hand with which to cope with even a minor drop in earnings or a modest increase in your costs. Clearly, it will not be a tenable situation. You must strive constantly to make a profit. However, once the revenue regularly exceeds the total costs, the business is profitable and, providing you do not allow costs to rise disproportionately to revenue, the venture will have become sustainable. From then on, the profit earned by the business will change only as the result of an increase or decrease in the demand for your service, or by an increase or decrease in the price you charge for performing it.

The point where the revenue of the business operation meets the total costs involved is known as the *break-even point*. Once you have calculated your total costs (fixed costs plus estimated variable costs) over a given period of, say, 12 months, you will know how much revenue you *must* generate in a year in order to break even. Revenue in excess of the break-even point is profit.

3.4   UTILISING TIME

The revenue of a service business, such as those listed in the previous chapter, is best calculated on the basis of what you will earn per hour. The number of hours in a year that you can devote to obtaining revenue should therefore be worked out.

Leaving aside Saturdays and Sundays, there are 260 days in a year. From this figure, you should deduct 8 public holidays, as well as, say, 14 days for annual holiday and, say, a further 8 days contingency for possible sickness. This totals 30 days, leaving you with 230 days per year for the conduct of your business.

If you decide to work, excluding meal-breaks, for 8 hours per day, you will have 1840 hours that you can devote to your work. However, for the reasons discussed earlier, only a proportion of these hours can, in practice, be employed carrying out *chargeable* work on behalf of your clients. This is because you must take account of time spent in travelling to and from your customers' premises, in promoting the business to get new customers and in dealing with the administrative tasks essential to the efficient running and control of the enterprise. Your *utilisation-rate* – that percentage of your working time for which you will actually receive payment – therefore plays a vital part in dictating the price (or fee) per hour, that you will charge for your service.

The point is best clarified with an example. If we assume that you require a minimum personal income from the business of £15 000 per annum and you believe that you can operate the business with total costs, other than your labour, not above £2500 per annum, then the revenue you will need to generate to achieve break-even, will be £17 500 a year. Let us also assume, for the purposes of illustration, that you anticipate a utilisation rate of 65 per cent, this will provide 1166 hours per year, in which you must earn the £17 500 essential to meet break-even. This means that you must achieve an average price (or fee) of £15 per hour.

Depending, however, on many factors, including the actual nature of your service operation, the size of your available market and the strength of the competition you will meet within the market, you may find that you can achieve a higher average price, say £20 per hour. Alternatively, you may be forced to accept a lower average price, say, £12 per hour. Whichever alternative applies, the utilisation rate you must achieve in order to break even will alter accordingly (see Figure 3.1).

The chart shows that to achieve break-even, you must earn £17 500 per year. At an earnings rate of £15 per hour, you will need to secure 1166 hours of work in a year, which is utilisation of 65 per cent of your total working time. However, if you can charge £20 per hour, you will reach break-even after only 875 hours, a utilisation rate of only 47 per cent of your total working time. On the other hand, where the prevailing circumstances permit you to earn, on average, only £12 per hour, it will take you 1472 hours to earn the necessary £17 500 a year, which requires a utilisation of 80 per cent of your total working time.

Using Figure 3.1 as your guide, you should produce your own break-even chart, to calculate the minimum hourly rate you will need to maintain, in order to achieve break-even in your busi-

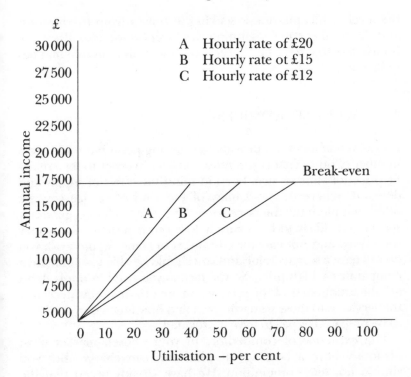

Figure 3.1 Utilising time

ness. As we have seen, however, whatever the price (or fee-rate) you subsequently arrive at, this will represent only the absolute minimum that you can charge for your service. All it will achieve is saving you from making a loss. It will not make you a profit and you will have to do much better if the venture is to survive.

The benefit of using break-even analysis, is that it provides the starting point to the setting of price. It also shows, in graphic form, the relationship between price (or fee-rates) per hour and the utilisation rate. In some service businesses, where the time that must be devoted to travelling, promotion and administration is minimal, utilisation rates in excess of 90 per cent may be achievable. In others, where there is a need for considerable negotiation with clients before assignments can be obtained, a rate above 50–60 per cent may be difficult to reach. Obviously, the level of income one is seeking to obtain from the business and the total costs of operating the business will also affect the hourly rate that must be charged and the utilisation rate that has to be maintained.

3.5 CALCULATING PRICES

Break-even analysis will provide the starting point but there are a number of other factors you must consider in order to set a realistic price for your service. Keep in mind the effect of supply and demand. Where the availability of the kind of service you are offering is plentiful, the price you will be able to charge, generally speaking, is likely to be relatively low. But if your service is very specialised and not easy for customers to come by, the work you do will have a scarcity value and you should be able to command a comparatively high price. So the factors you need to think about are the uniqueness of the service you are offering, how necessary the service is to those who will use it and how much they are likely to be prepared to pay to have it provided.

The existence of competitors in your chosen market must obviously have a bearing on what you can charge. But you should not fear competition. We have already noted that the presence of a competitor is proof that there is some demand for the service in the market, or he would not survive. You will need to take account of his or her price but not, necessarily, to copy it. Unless you already know a lot about the competitor, it would be wrong to assume that whatever price he is charging cannot be improved upon by the provision of a better quality service. The buying public well understands that it usually only gets what it pays for. There are always some people who accept a second-rate service at a low price because it is the best that they can afford. Others may well be able to afford a better service but have to accept the second-rate because no alternative appears to exist.

Another reason for not slavishly copying the competitor's price, is that you do not know what his costs are. Where you are competing against an established firm that has comparatively high overheads to carry, you may discover you can cream off some of his business by offering a slightly lower price and still make a very good margin of profit because your overheads are lower than his. Undercutting a competitor's price on this basis is entirely legitimate. If it attracts custom, it proves that your operation is the more efficient. You are providing like-for-like and doing so more cheaply because you are managing your costs better than he does. This is healthy competition.

Where price-cutting is to be deplored, is in a situation where you reduce your profit margin perilously close to your break-even point to gain work. It only needs the competitor to counter your attack by making a substantial cut to his own price, which you will be forced to match, to put you out of business.

One hears a lot about price wars between major product and service suppliers, particularly in times of recession, when the fight to hold individual market-share is particularly aggressive. But these are generally short-term ploys, undertaken to achieve limited marketing objectives. As a general rule, price-cutting is not good business practice and should be avoided as a means of countering competition. The best way to compete is not on price but on the quality of the service you provide.

Unlike the manufacture or sale of products, the provision of a service is highly dependent, from the viewpoint of quality, on the human element. As users of services ourselves, we all know this to be true. Price is frequently of secondary consideration when it is a choice between engaging the services of someone whom we like and in whom we have confidence or that of a person we do not care much for or whose competence we doubt. Anything that you can add to your service that provides additional benefit to customers improves its quality and should enable you to command a better price. Genuine concern and consideration for customers' interests – rather than the bland and often meaningless query 'is everything all right?' with which we are confronted by many service organisations these days – does not increase your costs. But it will often set you apart from competitors who do not bother with such niceties.

You should also be constantly on the look-out for other, practical ways in which to distinguish your service operation from those of your competitors. Anything that customers perceive increases the value of your service to them, will be reflected in the level of price they will be prepared to pay for it. It will also increase your reputation as a service provider and can tip the scale, more effectively than a lower price, when it comes to

obtaining future work. It will enhance your chances of getting
personal recommendation, the best way to secure new customers and far cheaper than the use of advertising.

Some people running service-type businesses base their prices
on their total costs plus a percentage for profit. Generally speaking, this is not the best way to do it. One should aim to charge
the highest price that one can expect to get, conceding a lower
price only where the circumstances make this necessary. There
is nothing in the least unethical about this. No one is compelled
to use your service. Those who do are as much constrained in
their choice by the market forces of supply and demand as you
are. They will buy what they consider to be an acceptable quality
of service for the best price at which they think they can get it –
and you, equally, are entitled to sell at that price.

There are some markets for services, where too low a price is a
disincentive, suggesting a cheapjack, or 'cowboy' type of operation, likely to produce shoddy work. Not every potential
customer shops around before ordering work to be done but
most have a fair idea of the going rate for such work and, very
often, a slightly higher price is seen as an assurance of quality
workmanship.

Circumstances, however, do alter cases and there will be times
when it may be to your advantage to offer a reduced price in
order to secure a particular job of work. You may find, for example, that during particular seasons of the year, demand generally
for your type of service slackens. You will have time on your
hands and the revenue flowing into the business is reduced. In
such circumstances, it is sensible to consider taking on work, if
it is available to you, at a lower price per hour than you would
normally charge, rather than have no chargeable work at all.

Bearing in mind that your fixed costs remain constant,
whether you are busy or not, any revenue that you can bring in
to the business at this stage will be better than no revenue. But
you must not work for nothing. The variable costs, that is to say,
the costs you will incur by actually carrying out the assignment,
such as petrol expenses or the short-term hire of special equipment, must be covered in the price that you charge. But you will
also want to make some contribution towards the fixed costs of
the business, otherwise it will not be worth while taking on the
work.

This is where the principle of distinguishing between your fixed and your variable costs helps you. It enables you to calculate a special low price on the basis of recovering all the variable costs involved in carrying out the work plus a percentage of your fixed costs. The actual percentage of your fixed costs you will be able to include in the price will, of course, depend on the level of price at which you can get the work. But in the absence of any more profitable use of your time, any contribution to your fixed costs that you can achieve must be worth while. It must be emphasised, however, that this is purely an expedient and should not be adopted too frequently. Your aim should always be to obtain work which will result in the full recovery of your *total* costs plus a margin of profit because this is the only way to sustain a healthy business.

Provided you remain alert to the risk element involved in the too frequent use of this expedient, there may be other circumstances where it could be in your long-term interests to offer a reduced price. Sometimes, it can be expedient to obtain work from a customer at a price below your normal rate because this will lead to more profitable work with this customer, or with others, thereafter. It is a 'sprat-to-catch-a-mackerel' approach, and where you see a genuine opportunity to increase your volume of profitable work it would be stupid to be too hidebound in your pricing policy. But once again, the cautionary note must be struck: be sure the opportunity is genuine and refuse to be dazzled by a spurious glint of promised riches into dropping your price unnecessarily.

3.6 FIXED PRICE WORKING

So far, we have discussed your pricing policy on the basis of a rate per hour because this is the most convenient way for you to ensure that you recover total costs plus a margin of profit that is as large as the market will bear. However, it is not always convenient to the customer if he is quoted in this way. For many types of service, the customer will want to know what the job is going to cost him. You can deal with this situation in one of two ways: you can either give him an *estimate* of the final cost, based on your calculation of the number of working hours involved, plus a percentage of time to cover contingencies, or you can offer him a fixed price. In practice, however, customers frequently interpret an estimate of the final price as the actual amount they will be required to pay. This can create a dangerous situation for you because, if you have underestimated the length of time the job will take, you could be out of pocket and faced with the difficult task of trying to get more money out of them.

It is an unfair situation but, if you want to retain the goodwill of the customers concerned and obtain future work from them, you will have to accept it. There are, however, ways in which you can minimise the effects of the problem. Make sure that your estimate of the length of time the job will take is reasonably accurate. The way to do this is to divide the work into sections. Where the nature of the task to be performed is complex, divide each section in to subsections. Estimate the length of time you consider necessary to complete each subsection so that you arrive at a figure for the completion of each section. Make a note of the period of time you are allocating to each section so that, once the work is actually in process, you will be able to monitor your performance against your estimate.

Where unforeseen circumstances have caused you to fall behind schedule, you face two alternatives. One is to extend your working day into the evening (or your working week into the weekend). The other is to explain the circumstances to your customer and get his agreement to a renegotiation of the job price to take account of the extra time necessary for its completion.

Apart from the loss of hourly earnings that may occur if a job overruns the time you have estimated, you will also have to consider the effect this may have on your availability to undertake subsequent work for other customers to which you are already committed. This may not be such a problem if your utilisation-rate is not much above 50–60 per cent of your total working hours, because, in a crisis, promotional and administrative tasks could be postponed. But if your utilisation rate has reached 80 per cent or more of your total working time, an overrunning job could seriously upset your timetable and give you problems with other customers. Careful time-estimating is, therefore, important both from the viewpoint of keeping customers satisfied with your service and of maintaining your rate of earnings.

Your working time as a service provider is the source of your income and, with this in mind, you must be on your guard against customers causing you to waste it. Whenever you are engaged on a job for which a fixed price has been established, ensure that any additional task you are asked to do is subject to an extra charge. To be accommodating to customers is an important part of any service but remember that every hour you give away for nothing represents an hour's-worth of revenue lost to your business.

Should you be asked to undertake work in the evenings or at weekends, you are entitled to apply an increased hourly rate. It is common practice in most service industries for staff to be paid time-and-a-half or double-time, for working so-called anti-social hours.

In the conduct of a service, there will be occasions when a client will expect you to purchase items on his behalf. If you are a garden designer, for example, part of your brief may include the ordering of plants and shrubs, paving or walling stone, or gravel for paths. Since yours is solely a service operation, all such purchases should be made on behalf of the client who will be responsible for making payment to the supplier. However, you do have the opportunity to add to your earnings by entering into an agreement with a local garden centre or builders merchant for the receipt of a commission based on a percentage of the value of the goods or materials supplied. What you must avoid, however, is any suggestion that you should purchase such items on your own account for subsequent reimbursement by the client on completion of the job. To do so would put you into a trading situation in which you would become personally liable to the supplier for payment for the goods. Should your client subsequently default in settling your account, or even delay payment for several months, you could find yourself in serious difficulties.

3.7 GETTING THE MONEY IN

Customers' unreliability in the matter of payment is a problem for all businesses, large and small. Provided you restrict your activities to the provision of a service and avoid all trading commitments, you will minimise your risk. The most you will stand to lose if you incur a bad debt will be the value of the time you have devoted to the work you have undertaken. However, this could still result in a major loss of earnings. In your situation, where you will be dependent on getting money in quickly to meet your commitments, even delayed payment by customers can create problems. For this reason, you must be specific about the terms on which you are prepared to perform your service.

If you provide a service direct to the public, you should receive payment as soon as the job is finished. Let customers understand, before you start the work, that you want prompt payment once it is completed. In the majority of cases you are unlikely to have problems. But you are bound to encounter some who will try delaying tactics and you need to be alert to their ploys:

- The customer's spouse or partner will pay the bill; unfortunately he or she has been called away urgently to Land's End or John o' Groats. As soon as they are back, you'll be paid.

- The customer says he is not entirely happy about some minor aspect of the work. It is not convenient to have you correct it today but if you call and deal with it next week, he will pay you then.

- There is another little job the customer would like you to do. The cost of it can be added on to the bill and he will settle up when you have finished it.

- The customer has simply not had a chance to get to his bank to draw out the money to settle your bill. Tomorrow? No, he cannot do it tomorrow. Or the next day, come to that. Leave it until next week and call in again. He will have the money ready for you.

- The customer tells you it is a funny thing but he cannot find his chequebook. But not to worry, it will turn up and when it does he will post the cheque off to you.

All the above excuses and many more like them are used every day by some of the most charming people you could wish to meet. Remember, however, that if the reason given for the delay is genuine, most customers will make a point of settling up with you in a few days. Beyond that, they are trying it on. Your response should be to press hard for your money and to do so persistently. You will not offend those who make a habit of such behaviour because they will be used to being hounded. If you make enough fuss, you will get paid, while others, who are more easy-going, will still be waiting for their money.

Where you supply a service to a business firm, on the other hand, it is likely that you may have to wait for thirty or more days before you can hope to get paid. Most commercial transactions are dealt with on the basis of account settlement within 30 days of the date of invoice or the 20th of the month following the month of invoice. Few firms will be prepared to settle more quickly, unless some special arrangement was agreed upon at the time the work was commissioned. Some companies may offer payment in seven days in return for a cash discount. This will, of course, reduce the amount of money you will earn for providing the service. If you are desperate to get quick payment, you could add the amount of the discount into the price you quote for the work but you would have to be sure that this did not make your price uncompetitive.

When dealing with business customers, indicate your payment terms in writing in advance of the work being undertaken. Once the job is completed, send your invoice promptly, restating your settlement terms. In advance of payment becoming due, send a statement, listing the invoice number, the date it was issued and the amount due for payment. If no money is received seven days after it is due, you are entitled to telephone the firm's accounts department, to ask when a cheque may be expected. Keep a note of all follow-ups, recording their date, the name of the individual you have spoken to and the gist of the conversation. Wherever possible, try to get a specific promise of when a cheque will be sent. Should it fail to arrive, telephone the person concerned, remind them of your previous conversation and ask that the cheque be sent immediately. Repeat the same exercise once more and if, again, no payment is made, you should write to the firm, enclose a copy of your statement and request immediate settlement. Should this fail to achieve a response, find out the name of the financial director or the managing director and make contact with this individual either by telephone or by letter.

3.8   DEALING WITH BAD DEBTS

Any further delay is likely to mean that you are faced with a bad debt. Your only recourse now will be to consider taking legal action. If the total value of the amount due to you does not exceed £1000, apply to your local county court for an explanatory pamphlet regarding the making of a small claim. This will tell you how you can issue a default summons against the offending company. The cost to you of issuing the summons will vary according to the size of your claim but it will not be excessive. Experience indicates that, in the majority of cases, firms in receipt of a default summons pay up quickly to avoid the stigma that attaches to having a county court judgement being made against them. It can jeopardise their prospects for getting credit facilities from other firms in the future.

If the amount of money you are owed is in excess of £1000, you cannot issue a summons through the small claims procedure of the county court. You must have recourse to the full court, a procedure that can be very expensive.

All forms of litigation are not only costly, they are liable to be extremely time-consuming. The wheels of justice turn slowly and you may have to wait for weeks, months, and in some cases years to recover a bad debt. For this reason, prevention is better than cure.

In the case of both private individuals and business firms, aim to minimise the risk, by getting initial payments from customers for part of the total cost of the work, wherever this is possible. If you have any doubts about a potential customer's reliability, make discreet enquiries before taking any work on. You are entitled, when dealing with a commercial organisation, to ask for references before accepting the offer of work because this is normal business practice. Write to the referees you are given and ask for their opinion on the credit-worthiness of the subject company, informing them of the monetary value of the impending transaction you have with the company.

The precept that you should take a firm line with customers to ensure their prompt payment is easy to recommend but often more difficult to apply. There is an inevitable dichotomy of interests here, in which you will find yourself being pulled in two directions at the same time. Wearing, as it were, your 'sales hat', you will be mindful of the need to maintain good personal relations with customers in the hope of obtaining future work from them. On the other hand, you will face the imperative need to get money in quickly, because you will have your own bills to settle.

It is a problem not peculiar to you. Every commercial undertaking faces the same difficulty. In medium and large-size firms, however, Sales and Finance are usually separate departments. This enables the salesperson to maintain a friendly relationship with the customer, while the accounts department deals with the nasty task of payment chasing! As a one-man, or one-woman, business, you will have to assume both roles. Bear in mind, however, that where your customers are commercial firms you need have no inhibitions about asking for your money once it is due. You can be certain that they are doing the same thing in respect to their own customers. So far as the work you do for individual members of the public is concerned, you are fully entitled to request payment once a job is completed, because this is a straightforward cash transaction.

All communication that you have with your customers will require tact on your part, and a firm, yet friendly, approach to ensure prompt payment should not cause offence. Indeed, the more businesslike you are in the way you treat your customers, the greater will be your credibility.

The obvious reason why you must get paid promptly is to maintain the flow of cash into your business. It cannot be emphasised too strongly that the control of cash flow is the most important aspect of managing your business. Many firms with full order-books have come to grief in the recession simply because they have had no money to hand when the time has come to pay their VAT or their suppliers of essential goods or services.

3.9   CASH-FLOW FORECASTING

The way to control the flow of cash into and out of your business, is to establish and maintain a *Cash-Flow Forecast.* This is done by listing all one's forthcoming financial commitments for a given period. This period should extend to at least three months although six months to a year would be better. Set down each item of expenditure that you know you will incur, where necessary estimating the amount involved and showing the date it will become due for payment. Similarly, write down, in date order of their likely receipt, the sums of money that will come into the business during the same period. Combine the two sets of figures to show, on a day-by-day basis, outgoing money and incoming money, together with the daily balance of cash in hand that this provides.

Whilst you will have little difficulty in estimating fairly accurately the amounts of money that will be going out of the business, you can have no advance assurance of how much cash will flow into your coffers in the weeks ahead; nor will you have any idea on which days particular sums are likely to arrive. Obviously, no forecast can provide an exact picture of the future. What it will tell you, is how much money you will *need* to receive and the dates by which you *must* receive it, in order to have sufficient funds available to meet those expenditure items you have listed on the dates you have specified.

A cash-flow forecast concentrates the mind on money problems that are lying in wait for you *unless you take appropriate measures to avoid them.* If the forecast indicates an imbalance, on a particular date, between the arrival of sufficient cash and the necessity to make a particular payment, you have only two choices. You can either attempt to get more cash in by that date or you can try to delay payment of the commitment. Since neither option may be open to you at short notice, the more advance warning you have the better.

The dates on which certain commitments, such as mortgage repayments and telephone bills, must be met, cannot be altered. But there will be other items of expenditure, both business and domestic, that you may be able to delay until further cash receipts from customers arrive. Ideally, you should keep some cash in reserve to meet urgent outgoings. But this may not always be possible and there will be times when you may have to juggle with your finances to keep your head above water. The arrival dates for customer receipts can at best be only an approximation, but the more clearly you can perceive a looming crisis ahead, the greater urgency it will give to your efforts to collect the money that is owing to you.

The inaccuracies inherent in such a forecast make it essential to update it regularly. You should make a point of checking it at least once a week, to take account of variations in your day-to-day current expenditure and the addition of further future commitments that have not been accounted for in the forecast, as well as changes that may have occurred concerning future cash receipts. The less predictable your particular business is, the more often you will find it necessary to amend or completely rewrite the forecast. It is very much a working document to which you will need to refer frequently, if you are to manage the money side of your business effectively.

3.10 SOURCING YOUR BASIC EQUIPMENT

The main problem in working for yourself without capital is to get the business up and running and to sustain it during its first year or two of operation. Once its financial viability can be proved, you will be able to consider your longer-term needs, particularly with regard to equipment. This will be the time to talk to your bank about possible loan facilities. Until that day is reached, when it comes to equipping yourself, you will have no option but to make-do-and-mend.

We have already noted that lack of capital prevents you from undertaking a manufacturing or trading type of business and confines your activities to the service sector. In providing a service, however, you will need equipment of one kind or another. For most of the options listed previously, the use of a telephone is necessary.

There are certain activities for which you will need the use of a car or small van. The provision of meals will require cooking facilities, with a refrigerator and freezer for storage purposes. Gardening and house decorating, too, will involve the use of tools and equipment of various kinds.

Most people already possess many such items. The majority of homes have a telephone. Large numbers of those who have suffered redundancy already own a car. Many householders, willingly or unwillingly, have involved themselves in DIY activities and possess decorating equipment and gardening tools. There are few domestic kitchens today that do not contain basic culinary equipment.

For certain types of service provision, specialised equipment may be necessary. In most towns there are hire centres for tools and equipment used in a variety of trades. They draw their custom not only from members of the public who have a repair or minor construction job to do at home but also from small service firms whose need of such equipment is only occasional and does not justify the tying up of capital that purchase would involve.

For most items of equipment, hire or lease rather than buy. If you have any small capital sum put by, hold on to it. You may need it in an emergency. Short-term hire charges generally are not excessive and can often be recovered by including them in the price you charge for the job. For the majority of service operations we have been considering, possession of a car or van is desirable and in certain cases it will be essential. Although most families have a car these days, the daily conveyance of children to and from school, as well as the need for a car, especially in rural areas, to make essential shopping trips to town, means that the vehicle may not be available for regular business use.

Among various options, leasing is a possible solution. The market for vehicle leasing has hitherto been restricted mainly to companies who operate fleets of cars. But there are signs that private motorists in this country may soon have the opportunity to follow the American approach to car acquisition by means of leasing. A number of major motor manufacturers are considering schemes to provide new cars on lease, with terms that are cheaper than hire purchase and may offer a better deal than a bank loan. If the service you decide to operate involves a lot of long-distance travelling, you will need a reliable vehicle. Leasing a new car over a two-year period and then buying it at a previously agreed special price, or merely returning it and entering into a further lease agreement for another new car, could provide the answer.

4 Finding the Customers

4.1 IDENTIFYING YOUR MARKET

Before you can attempt to get customers, you must find out if there are, in fact, any potential users for your service. Once you have established that they exist, your next step should be to discover what particular needs they have that can be satisfied by your service and how much they would be prepared to pay to have it provided. This question of customers' needs is of paramount importance. It is their needs and the extent of their desire to have them satisfied that will cause them to spend their money.

The need for various types of service provision varies widely. It is influenced by living standards, income levels and the geographical location of potential users. Over the past twenty years, income levels generally have risen sharply and this has raised living standards throughout the country. Many more people today are prepared to spend money for the provision of services that, in the past, they would either have gone without or would have provided for themselves.

All householders, for example, could be said to have a need for window-cleaning because windows get dirty and should be cleaned. The fact is, however, that we can divide householders, in this context, into three groups: those with dirty windows who do not care if they remain dirty; those who do care and clean them themselves; and those who do care, do not want to clean them themselves and prefer to pay a window-cleaner to do the work for them. If you want to promote a window-cleaning service, it makes sense to be able to differentiate between householders in your district who fall into each of these categories. You will not want to waste your time with the first two: you will need to concentrate on the third.

So, when we speak of the importance of identifying your market, what is meant is the importance of distinguishing that sector of a service market that comprises those who have a need for the type of service you propose to provide.

The work of identifying the market and its needs, calculating the number of potential customers and the level of price they would be prepared to pay for the service, is known as *market research.*

The first step in researching your market is to define its geographical boundary. If you intend a window-cleaning service, the geographical area of your market will be limited to a number of streets within your locality. But if you have decided to operate as a freelance commission agent, for example, acting for a number of manufacturing companies the area you propose to cover could extend to a radius of several hundreds of miles from your home.

The next stage is to establish in your mind the category of individual – or business firm – most likely to have a potential interest in the use of your kind of service. Set down on a sheet of paper the characteristics that will most closely define that type of person or that type of firm. For example, if you intend to provide a house history research service, prospective customers are likely to be confined to those who own property that is of considerable age and character and who are, therefore, more likely to be found in a higher than average income bracket. This is a service where the task of identifying the market is relatively straightforward.

A slightly more difficult market to identify would be that for family history research. Prospective users are certainly more likely to be found among those who enjoy above-average income. But they could just as easily be living in modern houses on up-market estates as in country mansions. Here, one would seek to identify them not so much by their location as by discovering the positions they hold in their particular trade or profession or within the local social scene.

Identifying the market for the provision of a floral display service, aimed at hotels, restaurants and those business firms that have somewhat prestigious reception areas, should not prove too difficult. Prospective customers can be easier to find in commercial markets because one can use what is known as *book research.* There is a vast amount of information available in this country to assist market research but gaining access to it is often expensive. But most people live within reach of a public library. In the reference section you should be able to find a lot of information that will be helpful. Most public libraries keep, for instance, a complete set of *Yellow Pages*, covering the whole country. Classified by commercial activity, each volume lists the names, addresses and telephone numbers of firms within the local telephone area.

Another useful publication to be found on public library reference shelves, is *Kompass*. This is published in two volumes. The first volume is indexed by product or service and lists the names of manufacturers, wholesalers and distributors. The second volume provides the addresses and telephone numbers of all the firms referred to in volume 1.

A further invaluable source of information is *Kelly's Manufacturers and Merchants Directory*. Entries are classified by trade and provide names, addresses and telephone numbers for thousands of firms, together with their trade descriptions.

If you have difficulty in finding the particular information you are looking for, have a word with the senior librarian. The majority of public libraries are now linked by computer and it may be possible for them to trace the source of the information you require by contacting other branch libraries within the local region, or indeed, nationally.

Having completed this stage of your research and obtained a fair idea of where the market for your service lies, you can then move to the next factor to be considered, which is the type of operation users require and the price they are willing to pay for it. The best way to do this is to study what your competitors are offering. Whether the type of service they currently provide is ideally suited to the needs of all their customers, you cannot yet know. But they do have the benefit of practical experience and you must presume that, despite any shortcomings in their performance, they must be obtaining a sufficient volume of the available market in order to stay in business.

If the service involved is one that is directed to consumers, as distinct from commercial firms, finding out what competitors are offering is comparatively easy. As a consumer yourself, you can make direct enquiries, posing as a potential client. Alternatively, if you prefer to remain anonymous, ask a friend to make enquiries for you. Consider in advance the kind of information you are seeking. This will obviously vary according to the nature of the service. Basically, what you need to know is the range of services the firm provides, what each of these consists of and the supplier's scale of charges.

In addition to what you can learn directly from competitive sources, you should also endeavour to obtain information from friends and acquaintances who have used the service provided by such competitors. Once again, formulate in your mind the questions you want answered, so that you can steer conversations into the right channels. Former users frequently express their opinion about the quality of the service they have received, its advantages and shortcomings, as well as their views of the firms that have provided it.

Where the service you intend to offer is directed towards commercial organisations, you can conduct your research by going direct to the user. The way to go about this is to select a number of firms whom you believe already use the kind of service you expect to provide and make contact with them. We shall consider later how you should approach potential customers. Business buyers of services often have a different set of priorities to that of consumers . If they use your kind of service on a regular basis, they are likely to be interested in finding out whether you can offer them a better deal than they are getting from their current suppliers. Provided that you know how to frame your questions, you should be able to learn a lot about their needs and how they would expect you to satisfy them.

Research of the market along such lines will inevitably open your eyes both to opportunities and to some of the difficulties you are likely to encounter if you decide to launch your service. In the light of what you discover, you may decide to modify certain aspects of your original plan. You may even decide, on reflection, that you should abandon this particular project and devise an alternative. Whatever the final outcome, research of this nature provides you with invaluable insight of the requirements of a market and the relative strength of the competition you will face, enabling you to make an informed judgement about the viability of a proposed venture.

The market is all-important. It is going to feed you and your family over the years to come. The more you know about it, where it is, what it consists of, its needs and idiosyncrasies and where it is heading, the better you will understand it and be able to serve it, thus securing your future.

In aiming to serve the market you have identified, think in broad terms, beyond the confines of your own specialised service. Look for the opportunity to supply additional services. Once you have established a connection with customers and won their confidence, there could be a variety of tasks you are able to perform that will satisfy other needs that they have. If you can do so it will expand your range, so that from the same limited group of customers, you will be able to extract a greater amount of revenue for the business without necessarily incurring an increase in costs.

4.2 PROMOTING YOUR SERVICE

Knowing the sector of the market where your customers are to be found provides a realistic basis for the next stage, which is to promote and sell the service.

There is considerable difference between the selling of a service and the selling of a product. Being tangible, a product can be shown to a potential customer before he or she buys it. Its appearance, quality and the value for money it represents, can be assessed before customers agree to part with their money. This cannot be done with a service. Until a service is actually performed, it does not exist. What is more, the quality of a service is never totally constant. How many times have you enjoyed a meal in a restaurant and liked the pleasant and attentive manner in which it has been served, only to return at a later date and been disappointed? This inability to demonstrate a service without performing it and being unable to guarantee its exact repetition makes the promotion of a service far more difficult than that of a product.

Because a service is intangible, its value and appeal can only be imagined by prospective customers. Therefore, the way to promote interest is to stimulate customers' imagination of it and of the benefits they will derive from using it.

Many people associate business promotion primarily with television and press advertising. This is, of course, where the bulk of the money allocated to publicity is spent by companies wanting to bring their products or services to the attention of the buying public. Any sum that you will be able to spare for advertising your business, however, will be extremely modest, but there are other avenues worth exploring that can help to promote your service where the outlay is small or non-existent.

The starting-point for any promotion is to gain awareness. You need to let it be known that your service exists. You require a pitch or platform where you can be seen and heard. If your market is local and your potential customers are members of the public, make contact with organisers of charity fund-raising events. Many such organisations hold open days and similar events to raise money and often welcome the support of local traders and suppliers of services, who take stalls and make a suitable donation to the good cause concerned. If the nature of your service lends itself, you could provide a demonstration and, having drawn an audience, distribute leaflets to bystanders.

Local organisations, such as Women's Institutes, gardening associations and sports clubs are always on the look-out for interesting speakers to address their meetings. Many towns have historical associations, whose members have a keen interest in the life of their district in former times. If your service is house or ancestry research, by addressing their meetings you will bring your activities to their attention.

Where a service is directed towards the business world, you could make contact with those responsible for organising seminars and conferences and offer a short talk on some topical aspect of your particular subject. Apart from the fees you may pick up from such performances, you will increase your credibility in the eyes of your audience by showing yourself to be an authority on your subject.

Advertising costs will add to the overheads of your business but should not be ignored because you need to spread the word and drum up interest in your activities. The most effective means of obtaining customers requires no financial outlay because it comes from the personal recommendation of satisfied customers. But until you have had the chance to obtain these recommendations, you will need to find other no-cost or low-cost methods of promotion. One way to get free publicity is to get a mention in the editorial columns of local newspapers. To sell their advertising space, editors need a constant supply of news items to attract readers. A newly-established local business is always potentially newsworthy. The same is true of trade and industry journals. So your first promotional activity should be the preparation of a press-release.

The way to do this, is to look at recent issues of your local newspapers to get an idea of how news stories are presented. Different papers have different styles of reporting but all such stories will be succinctly written, using a minimum of words in short paragraphs containing short sentences. When you draft your press-release, imagine yourself to be a press reporter and write in the third person. This will enable you to include your personal comments, using quotation marks: 'Mr. Smith, the proprietor, said that he planned to supply a comprehensive service. "There has been a lot of interest among local people," he added.'

You could also include any favourable comments made by your initial customers, especially if they are well known in the district. But ask their permission before quoting them. Find some aspect of your service that is particularly notable because this will make the story more interesting for the paper's readers and will give the report more the appearance of a news item, rather than an advertisement. You should also make sure that your trading name, together with your address, is included in the release.

Once the draft is completed to your satisfaction, have it typed with double spacing between the lines and with a wide margin on the left-hand side of the paper, to assist sub-editing. Put your name, address and telephone number at the top right-hand corner and head the story 'Press-Release'. Pictures are a useful adjunct to any news story. If you can get someone to take an action photograph of you engaged in performing the service, enclose it with the release, in an envelope addressed to the editor.

Where a service is aimed at commercial firms, it will be more effective to submit a press-release to the appropriate business journal serving the trade or industry with which your work is associated. Alternatively, you could telephone the editor and tell him or her about your activities. Before making the call, be sure to have a note to hand of the salient points about your venture, so that you can readily answer questions.

Apart from the fact that publication of a press-release costs you nothing, it helps to make potential customers aware of your existence. When you come to approach them directly, there is a good chance that they may already have heard about you as a result of the press exposure. But it is unlikely that a press-release alone will create a demand for your service. If the state of your finances will allow, some form of paid advertising will be helpful. This is where identification of your market gives you an additional advantage. You will be able to target your advertising message directly to those individuals, or firms, that your research has indicated to be most likely to have an interest in your service.

For a locally based consumer market, handbills pushed through letter-boxes are an economical form of advertising. They do not need to be expensively produced. A leaflet with illustrations and multi-colour printing is fine if you can afford it. But what is really important is the message: what it says and how it says it. From your own experience of receiving junk mail, you know that it usually gets only a brief glance before most of it goes into the waste bin. So the first thing to do, in drafting a handbill, is to be sure it will achieve four essential objectives:

- the words on the slip of paper must grab readers' attention before they destroy it;
- they must spark interest in the service you offer;
- they must arouse a desire to know more about it;
- they must motivate prompt action.

Whenever you scan the front page of a newspaper, it is the headlines you notice first. If none of them attracts your attention, you turn to the next page. It is the same with a handbill. If the headline makes no impression, the reader will throw it away. But if it arrests him he will read on. The headline needs to intrigue rather than inform. It can make a statement or it can ask a question. What it must do is catch the eye.

Below the headline, say something about the subject that the reader is likely to agree with. Few things are more compelling than to read a statement that encapsulates our personal views about a subject. Follow this with an equally succinct reference to your service and the specific benefits it offers. At the bottom of the sheet, tell readers to contact you immediately in order to learn more, and give your name, address and telephone number so they can do so. Figure 4.1 illustrates how these four objectives may be achieved with a handbill advertising a gardening service.

The cost of handbills will usually be cheaper than a newspaper advertisement containing the same message. What is more, you can control handbill circulation, by delivering only to certain districts or to specific streets, or even to particular houses.

Headline	GOING ON HOLIDAY? GREAT! BUT WHAT'LL HAPPEN TO YOUR GARDEN?
Sparking interest:	A really great holiday deserves a happy homecoming. Will yours be? At this time of year even a few weeks' neglect can turn the best-kept garden into a sorry sight to come home to.
Arouse desire:	But it needn't be! Our 'Happy Returns Garden Care Scheme' looks after your garden while you are away, with expert maintenance of plants, shrubs, lawns and hedges.
Urge action:	Make yours a Happy Return by phoning us today on ANYTOWN 1234 for full information. JOHN SMITH GARDEN SERVICES Anywhere Road, Anytown.

Figure 4.1 The essential points for an advertising handbill

Where potential users of the service are business firms a handbill will not be a suitable means of promotion. It is unlikely that you will be able to afford the expensive artwork and quality printing to match the standard of the majority of promotional material received by commercial organisations. But a cheap-and-cheerful effort will not do. It will smack of a miniscule budget and destroy rather than enhance your image. It will be better to forget the leaflet and concentrate on producing a really effective letter. This should be addressed to individuals in targeted firms, whose particular function suggests they are likely to be interested in the service.

The fact that it is to be individually addressed, conditions the style in which the promotional message should be couched. The use of a degree of razzmatazz may be appropriate for a handbill, pushed through the letter-box of an anonymous householder, but it would be out of place in a letter personally addressed to a company executive. Your objectives, which are to gain attention, evoke interest, create desire and motivate action, remain the same but the terminology you use needs to be somewhat more dignified and businesslike.

Start the message, this time, not with a headline but with an arresting sentence or short paragraph that will encourage your prospect to read on. Your second paragraph, once again, should seek to arouse interest, by making a statement with which the reader is likely to agree. It will indicate that you are addressing a problem close to his or her own experience, one about which you are like-minded.

In the third paragraph, tell him what you can provide that will solve his problem, by revealing the benefits that use of your service will bring to him and to those aspects of his company's activities for which he is responsible.

The final paragraph should urge him to action. If you want to go and see him, emphasise that you can explain the benefits of the service more fully by means of a face-to-face interview and will contact him by telephone in a few days' time to arrange a meeting. If it is not practical for you make a personal visit, you should invite him to write to you, or telephone, for fuller information. Figure 4.2 provides an example of the kind of letter one might send to potential customers to promote the service of a business training agency.

JOHN SMITH TRAINING SERVICES

Any Place
Anywhere

Mr John Brown
Nuts and Bolts Ltd
Newtown, Anywhere   4 February 1994

Dear Mr Brown,

Are your people rocking the boat?

Good relationship with customers depends on how *your*
staff react to *their* staff in difficult situations.
But when people find themselves under pressure, all
too often their emotions lead them into behaviour
that only makes matters worse. When this occurs, the
consequences can be disastrous.

Are you aware, however, that it is possible to train
staff to control their behaviour by adopting
positive emotional reactions to situations that
might otherwise become stressful? Based on research
of the emotional reactions of people at work, in
this country and abroad, techniques have been
developed enabling individuals placed in stressful
situations to be selective in their emotional
response and thus control their resulting behaviour.

This has positive implications for staff employed at
the customer interface and is the subject of a one-
day seminar I shall be conducting at the Grand
Hotel, Newtown, on 14 March entitled: 'STOP ROCKING
THE BOAT!' I am sure you will want key personnel
from your company to attend. The enrolment fee is
just £100 + VAT per person, reducing to £88 + VAT
per person when three or more attend.

This event has evoked considerable interest among
firms within the area and, due to limited seating
availability, early registration is strongly
advised.

Yours sincerely,

Figure 4.2 Letter to promote a business training agency

Having identified, by means of initial research, the firms you intend to circularise, you must find out the names of the individuals to whom these letters should be addressed. It is pointless addressing them to 'The Buyer' or 'The General Manager'. This tells the staff member who sorts incoming mail that your envelope contains yet more speculative advertising material. So much of this type of mail is destroyed on receipt. If your letter is to achieve anything, it must bear the name of an appropriate executive of the company.

Where you have previously worked in a trade or industry related to the service you are now offering, you may have existing contacts in some of the target firms. Alternatively, you may have other contacts who could suggest who you should write to. Failing this, you will have to telephone each of the firms on your list, explain briefly the nature of your service, saying you are writing to the company and ask for the name of the individual to whom your letter should be addressed. Sometimes, you will find that switchboard operators have instructions not to give this information but generally you will be given the name of someone who is a member of the firm's management. Since receptionists are not always entirely familiar with the particular functions of individual managers, you may find that the name you are given is not that of the person you really wish to contact. But your letter will, at least, get proper attention and will find its way eventually into the right hands.

This letter represents no more than a opening shot in your battle to win customers. Interest stimulated by your offer is likely to dissipate rapidly unless you sustain it by some form of follow-up. You may, of course, be lucky. One or more of the firms you write to may be on the point of using the type of service you are offering. It happens: but not very often. What is much more likely, is that a prospect reads your letter, thinks what you are offering might be useful, sometime. He might even raise the matter at a subsequent management meeting. But that is about as far as it will go – unless you do something about it.

In business, you have to make things happen. What you will have to do, in this instance, is to make personal contact with the individuals concerned. The time to do so is within no more than a week after your letters have been sent. If you leave it any longer, the recipients will probably have forgotten having heard from you.

What you need to know is whether any of these prospective customers has any interest in using your service in the form you have offered it or in some modified form. If they have no interest in your service whatsoever, you will still need to know this, so that you can remove their names from your list of prospects. The only way you are going to get answers to these questions is by talking to them.

You cannot force anyone to use your service if they show no interest, but you can, at the very least, try to persuade them to take an interest. If they will do this, it is possible that you may persuade them to use it. It is at this point in the promotion of your service that the personal selling aspect of working for yourself will confront you.

4.3 FEATURES INTO BENEFITS

Those with no previous experience of selling are often dubious about their ability to handle this side of their activities. The thought of having to sell something to others fills them with a sense of unease. They are likely to have convinced themselves that to be able to sell successfully one has to be a certain type of person, with personality traits that they themselves are lacking.

If you are to work for yourself you have to understand selling. The first thing to be clear about is that there are no such people as born salesmen or born saleswomen. Selling has nothing whatever to do with having the gift of the gab or being hail-fellow-well-met. On the contrary, to sell successfully one needs to be as good a listener as one is a talker. Obviously, to be able to communicate with other people is important; but effective salespersons are not necessarily highly sociable. Many are, in fact, quite the reverse in their private lives.

Selling is all about techniques and the ability to apply them selectively. It starts with knowing what it is one has to sell. In the case of a service, this means knowing, not just how it is performed but, more significantly, what it has to offer to those who use it. We have already touched on the subject of customers' needs. Every individual and every business firm has needs of various kinds. The precise nature of these needs varies from individual to individual and from firm to firm. The basis of effective selling is to recognise such individual needs and to present to customers those benefits the service has to offer that will most closely satisfy their needs.

Examine carefully your service 'package'. What are its features? Let us take, as an example, a home-sitting service, in which you provide 'minders' who will stay in the home of the owners to protect it and its contents during their absence. Among significant features of the service will be the care you take in your selection of suitable individuals to perform the minding role; your insistence upon the maintenance of certain standards of behaviour in the way they carry out their duties; the effectiveness of your control of these standards by your own regular inspections in the course of their tour of duty; any additional tasks that your 'minders' can perform for your clients, such as the care of pets, attending to routine garden maintenance such as watering or lawn-mowing, and the taking of telephone messages.

All of these features may be contained in the list of service functions you offer to customers generally. But not every potential client may have a pet to be looked after. Some householders may retain a gardener and will not want the house-minders to become involved with the garden. So not all the features of a service necessarily have appeal to all potential clients. However, the significance of certain features may not always be readily apparent to prospective users. It is only when they realise how a feature or group of features can provide a benefit that meets their needs, that they will warm to the idea of using your service.

So, instead of presenting the features of service merely as features, it is necessary to offer them as specific benefits, as though tailor-made to satisfy each customer's needs.

Let us look again at the list of features contained in the house-minding service and interpret the benefits that clients will derive from each of them:

FEATURE	BENEFITS
Careful selection of 'minders'	The house will be in the care of responsible, trustworthy people
Maintenance of high behavioural standards	No one other than the approved minders will enter the house in the owners' absence. No wilful or careless damage likely to furnishings or equipment. The house will not be left unattended
Your personal control by means of 'spot' inspections	Additional insurance against any lapse of set standards
Care of pets	Pets cared for in accordance with owners' instructions. They remain in familiar surroundings, avoiding stress that kennels or cattery could provoke. Cost of placing them in outside care is avoided
Garden maintenance	Plants watered and lawns mowed. Garden in good shape when owners return. Owners' time and effort to put garden to rights immediately on return thus avoided
Telephone message taking	Security of property enhanced because all calls answered. Messages noted for owners' return. In an emergency, arrangements can be made to alert owners at their holiday location.

Whatever the nature of the service you decide to provide, it will consist of features. To sell the service to prospective users, start by listing its features as we have done in the above example. At the side of each of them, write down the benefits it will offer to your clients.

The next stage is to look at the particular situation in which each client is placed to decide what his principal needs are likely to be. Assess how closely the benefits you can offer will meet these needs. When you are recommending your service to a potential customer, describe its features and then use three little words – '*which means that*' – to translate each feature into benefits that will be significant *for him*. For example: 'Our house "minders" are experienced in looking after other peoples' pets, *which means that* your cats will be properly cared for in your absence. You won't need to send them to a cattery, *which means that* you'll save money on boarding fees'.

This is the kernel of successful selling. It is understanding how the features of your service are translated into benefits and how the customer's situation indicates needs that have to be satisfied. By selecting the appropriate benefits to suit the needs, you are able to offer an attractive proposition.

There are, therefore, no hidden mysteries. Making a successful sale requires having correct information about the features of your service on the one hand and the particular circumstances of the customer on the other and interpreting both sets of facts accurately. Where problems will arise is where your facts are faulty or incomplete or where you are mistaken in your interpretation of them. To avoid or at least to minimise such difficulties, there are various precautions to take when selling your service to prospective users.

4.4   FINDING THE DECISION-MAKER

It will be a waste of time and effort, as well as travelling costs, if the individuals you approach are not in a position to make a decision regarding the use of your service. Where the service is directed towards the public, the decision-maker in a household could be either the man or the woman. Much will depend on the nature of the service. Very often decisions are made jointly by husbands and wives. But you will find that often the opinion of one or other member of a domestic partnership has a greater influence on the decision. For this reason, it is better to talk to couples than to individuals and to use the occasions to assess which person's views are more likely to influence their ultimate joint decision.

Where a service is aimed specifically at commercial organisations, the problem of identifying the decision-maker is more complex. When selling to a business firm, you have to direct your proposition to a person who has the authority to spend his or her company's money on the type of work you are offering to perform. Management titles are often misleading. Someone bearing the title of 'Buyer' or 'Purchasing Manager', is likely to be responsible for the placing of contracts with suppliers so far as the paperwork involved in the process is concerned. He may or may not have authority to initiate the commitments that such contracts involve. Services, particularly, tend to be specialised activities, affecting specific aspects of the overall management of a business. An office-cleaning service, for example, will be very much the concern of the office manager; a factory-cleaning service, that of the works manager. Their opinions as to what is required of such services will have a considerable bearing on a decision to use them. But whether either individual necessarily will have the authority to make that decision will depend on how the company is organised and to what degree buying authority is delegated by its directors.

So an important part of the selling process is to discover who is the right person to talk to. Sometimes, decisions are not taken by individuals but by groups of people, each of whom is liable to have a say in what is to be decided. Generally speaking, if a firm is very small, all decisions are taken by a single 'boss' figure who can be easily identified. But in larger organisations, there is often a 'pecking order' so far as authority to enter into commitments is concerned. Repeat orders for goods or services in regular use may often be issued by individuals at the lower end of the management hierarchy. Such people may also have authority to sanction low-cost purchases of items not previously used by the firm but for which a recognised need exists. The more expensive or unusual the purchase, the higher up the ladder it will have to go to be authorised.

Since every firm is differently organised, it is not always easy to know whom to approach. Switchboard operators and receptionists are usually helpful. But if the nature of your service is one not currently used by the firm, you could, in a large organisation, find yourself being shunted around and end up talking to someone in the wrong department. What is worse, however, is to end up in the right department but talking to the wrong person. Senior managers often delegate the task of interviewing would-be suppliers, of whom little is known, to junior individuals who act as go-betweens. When this occurs, one should take the opportunity to discuss the service in general terms, whilst endeavouring to learn something of the firm's current or potential use of the kind of service one hopes to offer. The conversation should be steered towards establishing the identity of the person who ultimately has the deciding voice in such matters.

Where the indications point to the existence of more than one decision-maker, it may become necessary to talk to all of them, either collectively at a meeting called for the purpose, or by individual interviews. This is only likely to happen in special circumstances, however, such as where one is offering a consultancy service which could have major financial or organisational implications for the client firm. In the majority of cases, the decision to use a particular service is likely to be reached by one, or at most two, members of the management team.

4.5 GETTING APPOINTMENTS

Getting to see people in positions of authority in business firms is not easy. With so many demands on their time, most executives are forced to limit the number of callers they will interview. Unless they can see some positive advantage to themselves and their companies in spending time talking to you, you will not get a hearing.

To keep unwanted visitors at bay, managers often use their staff to screen them from those attempting to get an interview. When you telephone a prospective client firm, the first of such screens you are likely to encounter will be the switchboard operator. She will probably have been instructed to deflect away from managers calls that could be time-wasting for them to deal with personally. You may be asked who you are and what it is you want to talk to the manager about. When you have said your piece, you are likely to be told that the manager is not currently available and that, in any case, he is always extremely busy. You will be advised to write to him. If you then point out that you have already done so and that you are attempting to follow up on your letter, you will no doubt be told that, if he is interested in your offer, he will be in touch with you.

Many people are successfully put off by this kind of rebuff. Do not become one of them. Ask to speak to the manager's secretary (or personal assistant, as many are now called). If you are told that she is not available either, at least get the name of the individual and ring later. It may prove necessary to repeat this exercise several times until, at last, you are successful and get to speak to her. Be careful to address her by name and explain you have written to her boss. Describe briefly the contents of your letter and say you would like to speak to him personally. Tell her why it is important, from his point of view, that you should do so. Give her some insight into the benefits that the service will offer him. If she says that he is not available to take your call, ask her if she will book an appointment for you. Many executives prefer their secretaries to maintain their diaries for them. You may or may not get an appointment at the first attempt. If you do not, you will have to keep trying until you do. Provided you leave a reasonable interval between each attempt and maintain a polite persistence, your efforts are likely to be rewarded.

4.6 UNDERSTANDING BUYERS' NEEDS

Before setting off to see a business customer for the first time, prepare yourself mentally for the interview ahead. Do not try to work out exactly what you are going to say. Remember that the person you interview will not have read the script and will not be giving you the answers you expect! What you need is not a script but a plan for the conduct of the meeting. This is because *you* will need to be in control of the discussion. You will have to take charge, setting the pace and the direction that you want the conversation to take. Unless you do this, it will not be you who is interviewing the customer but the customer interviewing you.

You will find yourself having to respond to him and to follow his lines of thought. You will not have the chance to persuade him to your view unless, from the outset, you take and maintain the lead.

Any plan must have an objective, a goal to aim for. In a sales interview, your aim will be to get the customer to agree to use your service. Along the route, however, there are subsidiary objectives to be met before you can hope to close the deal. Before you can effectively apply the benefits that are provided by the features of your service, to meet the customer's needs, you must first be sure that you know what those needs are. It is not only the buyer's decision-making authority that you have to consider. You have to take account of his personal characteristics, his situation within the company he is working for and his personal needs. Before you can conclude a satisfactory deal, you must not only satisfy the needs of his firm but his needs as well.

A commercial buyer carries considerable responsibilities and is often subject to many pressures. Any arrangement he enters into with you represents a commitment on the part of his company. It is a commitment shared, in varying degree, by both his superiors and his subordinates. Despite the assurances you give him about the quality of your service and the advantages his firm will gain by using it, he has to take your promises on trust. If your service and the manner in which it is provided do not live up to expectations, it is he who will get the blame.

For this reason there is often an understandable desire on the part of some buyers to leave well alone. If a company already uses your type of service, despite the fact that it may be costing more than you are proposing to charge, there will be a strong temptation for the buyer to stay with the devil he knows. Where the service you are offering has not previously been considered by the firm, he will need to be convinced of its value in order that he can convince others. His chances of doing so could be influenced considerably by the relationships he has with his peers and his superiors. His problem may not rest there. He may have to sell the innovation to his staff or his workforce, to secure their cooperation in its introduction.

These are but a few of the personal factors that can influence a buyer's reactions to your proposals. Until you meet the individual and have a chance to gauge the type of person and the type of firm you have to deal with, you cannot form any hard and fast ideas as to how you will conduct the interview.

4.7   DEALING WITH OBJECTIONS

Much is going to depend on what you already know about the company you are going to visit. If it is already using a similar type of service provided by one of your competitors, you can expect to meet with a resistance to change. The intangibility of a service, the difficulty in making any prior assessment of the quality of its provision, can make it far from easy to displace a 'sitting tenant', whose performance standards are already known to the customer. But this is an instance of where your knowledge of your competitors will be of help to you. One should never 'knock' a competitor. To do so is likely to damage your reputation more than it does his. But if you know the quality of his service and his standing in the trade, can recognise those aspects of his business where he is strong or where he is weak, you may find that there are benefits that you can offer the customer that he cannot match. In other words, where you have a competitive edge.

Every customer's situation is unique. Certain aspects of your operation that are satisfactory to one client could be considered unsuitable by another. Objections to your proposal are therefore inevitable but should not be seen as a sign of automatic rejection. A responsible buyer must be sure that in spending his company's money he does so with prudence. An objection is often a favourable sign, indicating that the buyer's interest has been aroused but he needs further clarification.

The best way to handle objections is to be prepared for them. Before going to sell your service, make a list of possible circumstances that could cause the buyer to raise objections to your proposal. Then consider each likely objection and decide how to counter it. Some potential objections are so predictable that the best way of dealing with them is to raise them yourself before your customer does. By removing as many doubts from his mind as you can you will hasten the moment when you can close the deal.

Never fear an objection. Those you have not anticipated need to be brought to the light of day because they reveal doubts that still linger and, until you remove them, the customer will not be sold on your proposition. An objection indicates a need that has yet to be satisfied. Only when all his needs are catered for by the benefits you offer will he be satisfied and accept your proposal.

An interview of this kind will normally open with a short exchange of pleasantries, enabling each party to quickly size up the other. Then you must take control of the situation and get down to the reason for your visit. It is important at this early stage to get the buyer talking, so that he can reveal something about himself and his company. The best way to do this is to ask a question, one that is open-ended and cannot be answered by a simple 'yes' or 'no'. You will want to find out if he uses your kind of service and if not, why not. He may respond by saying that he does not need your service or that he already uses the service provided by a competitor and has no wish to change. Either objection needs to be politely challenged. Get him to tell you why he does not need the service or why he does not want to change. The reasons he gives will show you how he is thinking and, if they are insubstantial, they may give you the opportunity to present your case and change his mind. If they have some validity, however, you may need to broaden the area of the discussion to include considerations he may not have taken into account. This is where the specific benefits you have to offer need to be emphasised. You are giving him new information that he may need time to think about.

Keep in mind that what you say, and how you say it, reveals much of your character to him. He will be assimilating knowledge of you that will influence his reaction to your proposals. Remember too, how important it is to be seen to listen. The customer will have a point of view and it is vital to your interests to hear it. One encourages talk on the part of another by what is known as 'active listening'. Let the other person know that you hear what he says and are in harmony with his thoughts. Summarise the buyer's remarks in your own words, showing him that you have correctly interpreted what he has said. Keep eye contact with him while you are talking and when he responds. Body language is persuasive. If you appear relaxed it will encourage relaxation in him. His bodily posture and physical movements will often say more about his reactions than his actual words.

4.8 GETTING A DECISION

Closing the deal depends on removing all the customer's objections. Once you believe you have done so, the time has come to attempt to close. Sum up the situation, in a way that implies that all problems now appear to have been removed and that he is ready to accept your offer. If he seems to agree with what you have said and does not raise any further objections, you should immediately close the deal. If he does not agree with your summary, however, and does raise a further query, it will indicate that he has still not yet made up his mind. Deal with this additional objection, get his confirmation that this is no longer a problem for him and repeat the attempted close once more.

Sometimes, a point is reached in the discussion where the buyer can find no further reason why he should not agree the deal, yet has an emotional reluctance to do so. Logically, he knows the deal is right for him but he hesitates to make the commitment. This is where you, the seller, must make the decision for him for his own good. Take it upon yourself to suggest when the service should be provided and the actual date when the work will start. Show him by your attitude and behaviour that it is your understanding that a deal has been struck and that he wants you to go ahead. If you have misread the situation he will tell you so *now*. If he does not do so, you have his tacit agreement and can proceed accordingly.

4.9 CUSTOMER GOODWILL

Getting customers is one thing; keeping them is another. However hard you try to prevent it, sometimes things will go wrong and customers will be less than satisfied with your service. When this occurs, remember that customers' goodwill is one of your most valuable assets. The effort to maintain it may often have to take priority over other matters. If you upset a customer, for whatever reason, and do not repair the damage promptly, you stand to lose a lot more than the value of any future work he may give you. People talk and one person's ill will can fuel gossip that can seriously damage your reputation.

A service operation is a package of benefits in which attention to the particular concerns of the customer plays a major part. This is where the single operator can score over larger firms. One of the biggest problems facing corporate organisations is the erosion of custom that results from the careless or ill-mannered behaviour of staff. When you work for yourself, it is entirely up to you whether your customers are pleased or displeased with the treatment they receive. Most of the problems that arise in providing a service result not from any calamitous failure to perform the work itself in a satisfactory manner, but from a lack of consideration for customers' feelings.

The emotional needs of customers should never be disregarded. They always have a profound effect on their choice of a supplier. It is very easy to become irritated by what appears to be customers' petty demands or anxieties. But the better attuned you are to what concerns them, the easier it will be to retain their goodwill and give satisfaction. In practical terms this means quick response to enquiries; keeping them informed of the on-going situation, particularly where there are unforeseen problems or delays in completion of the work; and maintaining a tolerant and considerate attitude to their doubts and fears.

Just one example serves to illustrate the point: the returning of customers' telephone calls. It costs little, in both time and money, to ring someone back, even if you do not have the answer to their query. They then know they are not forgotten, that you are trying to be helpful. The gesture will not be unappreciated. Remember that it is the small things that often count most in human relationships.

There will be occasions when you will want to turn work away. You may have enough booked already and to take on more will lead to a deterioration in the standard of work you want to maintain. Alternatively, the job you are offered may be too complex for you to undertake satisfactorily. Or the job may be too small to be worth while, or too big to handle. The customer could be a person you dislike and it would be best for all concerned if you did not do work for him. The offer of work may have come from a commercial firm whose payment record you have heard is suspect and you do not want to get involved.

These are all valid reasons for turning work away but sometimes one has to take a long-term view of a situation. The attitude you adopt with a customer can affect your relationship with him for years ahead. Circumstances change. The work you do not want today could be useful to you at a later date. Even the firm with the doubtful payment record could in time resolve its financial problems and become a worth-while prospect. So you do not want to burn your boats by rejecting current offers of work in a manner that might give offence.

There are a number of ways in which to handle such a situation. You can say that you are fully committed at present but would be glad to undertake the work later on if the customer's need is not urgent. This response is likely to create a good impression by implying that your service is highly regarded. Alternatively, you can quote a price you know to be higher than competitors would charge for the work and hope that the customer will go elsewhere. Of course he might accept your price. If he does and you find yourself committed, the work will at least show you an improved return which could compensate for some of the problems you expect to incur. But the danger of attempting to out-price yourself is that you could become labelled as uncompetitive which would be damaging to your reputation.

Where the nature of the work offered is technically beyond your capacity or involves the use of equipment or other resources you do not possess, your best course could be to say so and recommend one of your contacts in a similar line of business to yourself who is capable of doing the work satisfactorily. Be sure to let the person concerned know of your referral. It may prompt him, on another occasion, to return the compliment and put work your way that he may be unable to handle.

In circumstances where you think to turn work away because you are currently overloaded or where the technical requirements are too onerous, there is an alternative to letting the job go elsewhere. You can apply a networking arrangement. Networks consist of groups of freelance operators who normally work on their own and are, therefore, of independent status. They join forces as occasions require and pool their resources to undertake jointly work that none would be capable of tackling on his own. Where you have contacts among other self-employed people who have skills suitable for the work, you could invite them to join with you to do the work on offer. Agree between you a price to charge the customer and decide how you will subsequently divide the profit. In this way, you retain the customer by satisfying his needs. Obviously, care must be taken in your choice of co-workers because you will remain responsible to the customer for the quality of the work done.

4.10 THE TELEPHONE IN BUSINESS

No form of business communication is likely to be so effective as that which results from personal contact. But travelling to visit customers is time-consuming and expensive, particularly if one's clients are widely dispersed. Using the telephone is the best alternative. This, too, can be costly, but you will be able to maintain contact with far more customers by telephone than will be possible by travelling round the country. What is more, if you are constantly away from base, customers and potential customers will find it difficult to contact you. Admittedly, car phones can meet this need but they involve a further expense you may not be able to afford in the early days.

People who rely heavily on the telephone in business will confirm that it is possible to build a close relationship with a customer by telephone, without ever meeting the person concerned face to face. When talking to someone on the telephone it is surprising how quickly one forms a mental picture of them, by their tone of voice and its inflections, their use of words, their pace of speech. The more frequently one has occasion to speak to the same person, the easier it becomes to recognise their mood and to detect their reaction to the trend of the conversation. Their uncertainty, caution, anxiety, even their suspicion comes across very clearly, as does their sincerity, enthusiasm and friendliness.

When using the telephone in business, you will want to give the impression of being a well-organised person who is likely to prove reliable. You never know exactly when customers are going to ring you and what questions they may ask, but you can anticipate many calls, especially if you have been actively promoting your service and have invited enquiries. Keep a notepad beside the telephone for messages and with it your price list and details of your service, if these are at all complex. You can then answer queries in a positive manner. Always ask for the personal name of a business caller as well as the name of their firm and get their telephone number for phoning back.

Remember that incoming calls do not cost you anything except time! Since the caller has displayed sufficient interest in your service to have taken the trouble to ring you, use the opportunity to find out as much as you can about his particular needs and tell him of the benefits that your service can provide.

When using the telephone to make sales calls, advance preparation is very important. A telephone call differs in many respects from a personal visit to a customer at his house or place of business. If he has agreed to see you by appointment, you can usually expect to have a reasonable period of time – fifteen minutes to half an hour – in which to have your say. At the time of the visit, however, you may find the customer under pressure. His attention to what you are saying could be distracted due to interruptions by others. Being on the spot and aware of what is occurring, you will be able to react appropriately, but when you ring someone up, your call reaches them 'out of the blue'. It is an interruption to what they are currently doing. You do not know what minor crisis you have intruded upon.

It is important to bear in mind that when a customer takes your call he probably has other things on his mind. It may take him a moment to adjust his thoughts. Give him that moment, by speaking clearly and not too hurriedly. Explain who you are and – where this is possible – link your name to something that will help him to 'place' you, such as a letter you may have sent him recently or a reference to your activities that may have appeared in the local or trade press. If a mutual acquaintance has suggested that you call him, tell him so immediately. Many people have an instinctive resistance to a call from a stranger. It is a form of anxiety and you need to remove it quickly because until you do you will not achieve a sympathetic response. Be friendly and smile as you speak. It is a recognised fact that one's tone of voice reflects one's mood when speaking on the telephone.

Before dialling, be certain what it is you want this call to achieve. Write down on a piece of paper the main points you want to get across. Think of the possible objections that the client may raise to whatever you intend to propose and be ready to answer them. Being equipped enables you to speak with greater assurance, remain relaxed and in control of the conversation.

If your service business involves a lot of routine communication, you should consider getting a facsimile machine. This can, if you so wish, be rented in the same way as a telephone instrument, from British Telecom. Models are available that operate on the same line as your telephone, thus avoiding the cost of having a separate line installed. The speed of transmission of a fax message, written on A4-size paper, is measured in seconds and is very much cheaper than giving the same amount of information over the telephone. Another advantage of using fax is that a message, personally addressed to a business executive, will reach him in exactly the form in which you have written it, whereas a verbal message left with a secretary is liable to be distorted in the retelling or may not be delivered at all.

Most commercial firms are on fax these days and, apart from the time saved, the cost of sending a fax message is cheaper than second-class mail. Furthermore, it is quite acceptable to send a handwritten fax message to a company, whereas a handwritten letter would give a very unbusinesslike impression.

Because of its relative cheapness and speed of transmission, many firms now use the fax message as a means of canvassing prospective clients. Such messages do not have the visual appeal or persuasiveness of a well-designed, colour-printed circular. But if the content of your message is sufficiently arresting and is likely to be of practical interest to the reader, you can unashamedly fax it to the most up-market of your potential customers. When used for this purpose, the message should be typed on your headed paper and personally addressed to the intended recipient.

A telephone answering machine is another very useful piece of equipment you may want to consider, especially if your work takes you away from your base for much of the time. Suitable machines are not expensive to buy outright or you can, like the fax, rent one from British Telecom.

5 Getting Organised

If you decide to work for yourself without capital, the only investment you can make will be that of your ability and the time you expend in utilising it. Time is therefore an irreplaceable resource that you cannot afford to waste. The more organised you are in the way you run your business, the more economical will be your use of time.

5.1. ORGANISING YOURSELF

To be organised in business you have to start by organising yourself. In your alloted twenty-four hours a day, you have to sleep, eat and work. You cannot increase the availability of time but you can make the time at your disposal more productive.

It is an important consideration because, whatever the type of service operation you decide upon, there will be three distinct activities that have to be performed:

- getting new work to keep the operation going;
- dealing with the administration of the business;
- performing the particular service.

Time spent on the first two items will not earn you a penny. Only the proportion of your total working time actually spent providing the service can be charged to customers.

As a percentage of your working time, your utilization-rate will vary according to the nature of the service you provide. In business consultancy, for example, the utilization-rate achievable by a sole practitioner in his or her first few years of operation is unlikely to exceed fifty per cent. This is because a considerable amount of time will be occupied in finding new clients, discussing the detail of potential assignments and preparing proposals to win contracts. Regardless of the type of service business you eventually settle upon, you will find the task of promoting it will be time-consuming. Nor will you be able to avoid spending time on administration. The bookkeeping function must be main-

101

tained to ensure that customers are billed promptly for the money they owe you, that your own business commitments are kept under proper control and that payments due to your suppliers are made on time. By organising your use of time, you will reduce its waste and thereby increase your utilization-rate, with a corresponding improvement to your income level.

Using time economically does not mean cutting corners. Allocate time as you would any other resource: on the basis of what you consider sufficient for the task to be done. It is inevitable that one should prefer to tackle some tasks rather than others; those that are least agreeable tend to be put to one side. For many people in business, paperwork falls into this category. Documents reaching them through the post tend to be briefly scanned on arrival and to be consigned to an in-tray, to be dealt with at a later date. By the time that 'later date' finally arrives, the tray is usually overflowing. They are then faced with a monumental task of sifting and sorting, of reading and belated action-taking. The time consumed in doing this is vastly greater than the few minutes each day it would have taken to deal with items individually when they first arrived.

What is even more to the point, such paperwork usually consists of invoices for items purchased, copies of invoices sent to customers and general correspondence, which may need to be referred to quickly during the course of the day-to-day activities of running the business. If a specific item is not easily to hand, further time must be wasted looking for it. Worse still, decisions are likely to be made, and risks taken, without reference to the essential facts, because the sheet of paper on which they are written cannot be found.

The way to avoid such a sorry state of affairs will be to start your business in the way you want it to continue. There will be many minor yet essential tasks that will take only a few minutes to complete and should be tackled strictly on a daily basis. Time and effort are also saved by having a recognizable place for everything you use in the course of your work. Make it a habit to put things away after using them so that you can find them quickly the next time you need them. You should also maintain a jobs-to-be-done list. It is surprising how many people who consider themselves to be businesslike fail to do this. They seem to believe they can remember the hundred-and-one things that have to be done in a business, week-in and week-out. Take a sheet of ruled A4-size paper, staple it to a piece of cardboard and enter on it all the things you have to remember to do. As you deal with each item, cross it through. Every time a new item arises, add it to the list. Make a habit of checking the list first thing each morning and again in the evening when you finish the day's work. Give priority to urgent matters. Then tackle the items that you least like having to deal with. Get them out of the way. The pleasant tasks left on the list will get done without undue effort, simply because you will enjoy doing them. All this may sound very elementary and so it is. But organising your time is all about self-discipline and it has to start at an elementary level.

Awareness of the need to use your available time productively is only one aspect of getting organised before you start your business. It is equally important to have a realistic plan of action. Just as muddled methods of working will waste your resources of time and effort, so, too, will muddled ideas of where you want to go and how you expect to get there waste your energy and wrong-foot you at every turn.

5.2 A BUSINESS PLAN

Those who voluntarily opt out of employment, in order to set up in business for themselves, are always advised to prepare a business plan. This is regarded as an essential document for presentation to one's bank manager when seeking an overdraft or loan facility. But the real value of such a plan is that it compels those who have prepared it to consider in detail the full implications of their proposition. For this reason, you should take time to draft your own business plan, even though you do not intend to seek your bank's assistance.

Since your plan will be for your own use and not for that of anyone else, think carefully of what should go into it. Its essential purpose will be to make you think forward. It should force you to decide how you will deal with circumstances that may arise. Whatever you plan to do when you start your business can only be based on your current perceptions. Subsequent events and your increasing experience may prompt you to deviate from the original plan. But this does not negate the need for it. On the contrary, should you make a decision to alter one aspect of your planned activities, you will do so in the knowledge that the overall pattern set out in the plan is going to b disturbed. You will find yourself having to take into account other factors that are going to be affected by your proposed amendment. In other words, you will have to consider the total effect that your proposed alteration will have on the future course of the business. The plan therefore provides another means of self-discipline by encouraging you to make decisions that are based on a realistic consideration of the facts, rather than acting on impulse.

The ingredients of a business plan can be divided into four main sections, the first of which concerns yourself. You are the human ingredient, the person whose abilities and characteristics will influence how the business will be run. You will already have undertaken a personal audit of your strengths and weaknesses. This should go into the plan to indicate the capability that your presence will bring to the enterprise.

The second section is about the resources available to the business. Leaving aside financial investment, which will not apply, consider what will be available for use by the business: part of your home as accommodation for the business; a car or van; equipment, such as a telephone, a typewriter or a copier; tools of a trade, where this is relevant, for use in providing the service. There may be other resources, necessary for the conduct of the business, that are not immediately available and will have to be acquired. These, too, should be itemised, with an indication of how you propose to obtain them.

The next section relates to the market you are proposing to enter: who will buy your service and why should they do so? The findings of your market research should be entered here because it will substantiate your belief that there is a genuine demand for the service. Set out the geographical area of the market you plan to cover. Indicate the prices you intend to apply. Identify those firms currently operating in this area of the market who provide the same or a similar service and set out the reasons why you believe you will be able to compete with them satisfactorily.

The final section of the plan has to do with the financial aspect of the proposed business. Since its primary function will be to provide an income for you and your dependants, you should calculate how much money you will need to draw each month to maintain an acceptable standard of living. To do this, you will have to examine your personal finances in detail to arrive at an acceptable figure. Such drawings will form part of the anticipated costs involved in the running of the business and which will need to be covered by the intake of revenue, in the form of fees charged for the service.

Also in this section you should include your cash-flow forecast of money coming into the business in the form of payments received from customers, and the outflow in the form of payments you make to settle bills for purchases on behalf of the business, as well as your personal drawings. Of course, until you actually start the business, you will have no idea when the inflow of money from customers will begin or what its value is likely to be. You have yet to find these customers, persuade them to use your service; you have to provide it and then collect the money. This means that you will have to make an assumption. Look again at the market research you have undertaken. How many of the potential customers you have identified do you realistically expect to use your service in your first month of operation or in the first three months? If you can come up with a figure and you relate this to your proposed charges for the service, you should be able to estimate the amount of cash that will become due to you. As far as the likely outflow of cash is concerned, this should be much easier to predict because the bulk of it will relate to your personal needs.

The purpose of a cash-flow forecast is that it provides a picture of how you are likely to stand at any future time so far as the availability of cash is concerned. Neither you nor your business can survive without recourse to available cash. The tricky part about controlling cash flow, even for well-established businesses, is that one never knows precisely when incoming sums of money will actually arrive. Not only does it depend on the amount of work that the business has been able to undertake during any given period of time: it also depends on when customers decide to pay. The problem is far less acute for a purely cash business, such as a retail shop, where customers make immediate payment at the time of the transaction. Where it is necessary to extend credit to customers, however, there will always be uncertainty about when payment will be received.

Should you find, when you come to draft your plan, that you have insufficient facts about your proposed business – particularly with regard to the market and the financial aspects of the enterprise – it will indicate that your research has not been sufficiently thorough. This is the value of preparing the plan. It highlights any weakness in your proposition, forcing you to revise your estimate or, if necessary, to undertake a complete rethink, before you commit yourself. If, despite your best endeavours to make them do so, the facts do not add up, the chances are that you do not have a viable business idea and you will have to think again.

Where you are able to complete your plan to your own satisfaction, it will be prudent to try to get a second opinion. If you have, among your personal friends or close business acquaintances, someone whose commercial judgement you respect, show him your plan. He may be able to come up with helpful suggestions. If queries are raised to certain aspects of your scheme, this could also be most useful because the time to amend your plan is before you set about putting it into operation.

5.3 CHOOSING A NAME

Once you have decided on the type of business you intend to run, you will need to give it a name. It is worth spending a little time over this because there are a number of factors to be considered. Some people are content just to use their own name, with a brief reference to what they do:

John Smith   Window Cleaner

Others prefer to use their initials:

JBS Gardening Services

The alternative is to use a made-up name:

Vista Garden Design

In deciding on an effective name for your business, take account of the following:

- it should attract attention
- it should have pleasant rather than unpleasant connotations
- it should tell people what type of service you provide
- it should be easily pronounceable
- it should not be capable of being confused with the name of another locally based or a nationally known business
- it should be a name that is easy to remember

The only value of using your own name is if you are already well known in your local community and you intend to serve a locally based market. Similarly, if your market is within a trade or industry in which you have been employed and your name is widely known among business acquaintances, it could open doors for you more readily than if you were to trade under the disguise of some other name.

Generally speaking, the use of initials as a trading name is unwise. The entire world appears to be awash with alphabet soup these days! A trading name consisting of initials is not merely boring, it is often confusing or meaningless.

If you decide to make up a name, keep it short, attractive-sounding and easy to say, as well as appropriate for the type of business you are operating.

There are many firms that provide services to their local community who receive much of their custom as the result of potential users looking them up in *Yellow Pages*. Since entries in these directories are arranged alphabetically, remember that it is better to have your trading name appearing up among the As and Bs rather than at the end, with the Ys and Zs!

As a sole trader or a partnership, you do not have to register the name you give to your business. However, if it is a made-up name, your own name must appear on your printed letterheads and your invoices. Furthermore, if customers or suppliers have access to the premises where you conduct the business, the trading name has to be prominently displayed.

5.4   TRADING STYLE

Before you can consider the other matters that have to be attended to in setting up the business, you must first decide the form in which you intend to trade. There are three options:

- as a sole trader
- as a partnership
- as a private limited company

With no capital sum at risk in the business and the unlikelihood of your running up any major debts with suppliers – as might occur in a manufacturing or trading business, such as a factory or shop – you will not need the protection that limited liability status provides. Nor are you likely to have available the necessary funds to acquire such status. Your choice, therefore, lies between trading as a sole proprietor and as a partnership.

The merits of entering into a partnership agreement are usually twofold. Where each partner introduces capital to a business, the total sum available for trading purposes is greater. In addition, the management of the enterprise is strengthened because two or more people have a vested interest in its success and their combined contribution of knowledge, skills and experience will be greater than those of a single proprietor.

Where one intends to work for oneself without capital, however, the financial advantages of working with partners does not arise. So far as the skills contribution of partners is concerned, one does not have to enter into a partnership arrangement in order to acquire such an advantage. Should you have occasion to need the advice or practical assistance of others, these can be obtained by other means. You can commission the services of others on a fee-paying basis as and when required or you can sub-contract part of an assignment that you are unable to handle yourself. The other alternative is to make use of the network system that has already been described.

Working for oneself without the availability of capital will place a heavy strain on the personal relationship of a sole proprietor and his or her nearest and dearest. To attempt a business on this basis in permanent alliance with another individual *facing similar pressures* could be a recipe for disaster.

5.5 KEEPING THE BOOKS

For many self-employed people, the paperwork side of running a business is often the most irksome. If one is trading, as distinct from providing a service, the need to keep accurate stock records and to account for VAT can be a time-consuming and tedious chore. In the case of most service operations, however, and particularly where the annual turnover is below the VAT threshold the essential records that must kept are fewer and easier to maintain.

The important thing to bear in mind when devising a records system is that it should be simple to operate. It has only one basic job to do: to give you the facts about your financial situations quickly, whenever you need them.

Something you will constantly need to know is what it is costing you to run the business, so that you can decide what to charge for your service. As we saw when discussing pricing policy, some costs are fixed and some are variable. But the value of fixed costs, the permanent overheads of the business, does not remain static and over time will increase as the result of inflation and by the possible addition of extra overhead items. The salary you draw from the business is likely to be its biggest overhead and you will need to know whether the business is earning enough to be able to sustain this cost at its current level. Alternatively, when the volume of work you receive from customers expands, you may be led to believe that, as a result, you can pay yourself more. Before doing so, however, you will need to be sure that the increase in business turnover is, in fact, producing an increase in profits.

This is an important consideration, because being busier does not necessarily mean that you are earning more money. The greater your business activity, the greater will be the variable costs in respect to items such as fares or petrol usage, incurred as a result of increased travelling. Knowing whether you are running at a loss, just breaking even, or actually making profits, is essential for the responsible conduct of the business. Without such knowledge, for example, you cannot decide whether you can afford to quote a reduced price to attract extra work during a slack period.

Quite apart from your need of accounting information for the proper control of the business, you will have to know your receipts, expenses and resultant profit (or loss) figure in order to complete your annual income tax return. The details that show how these are arrived at need to be readily available, should you be required to justify them.

The number of account books you keep should be kept to a minimum. As a one-man or one-woman operator, you simply will not have the time to devote to any complex bookkeeping system. Nor will you need it. All you need to record are:

- cash movements in the form of receipts and payments;
- the value of invoices sent to and payments received from account customers;
- the value of invoices received from and the payments made to suppliers with whom you have an account.

On the assumption that you will be operating a service business, with an anticipated turnover below the threshold for VAT, a simple *cash book* should be sufficient for recording all your cash transactions. For small, miscellaneous purchases, including items for which one does not normally obtain a receipt, use petty cash vouchers and enter the serial number and value of each voucher in the expenditure column of the cash book.

Ready-made books of account are obtainable from stationery shops but they are relatively expensive. You can save yourself money by adapting an ordinary ruled exercise book. Using facing pages, record receipts on the left-hand page and payments on the right. Divide the pages into columns suitable for the details you wish to record. Figure 5.1 provides an example.

If the nature of your business is such that all sales and purchase transactions are conducted on a 'cash-on-the-nail' basis, the entries you make in the cash book will be a sufficient record. However, where you give or receive credit, you will need a means of keeping track of customers' payments, as well as the payments that you are due to make to your suppliers. The best way to do this is to keep sales and purchases ledgers. Once again, you can save money by producing your own. A loose-leaf system is preferable, because the details relating to each customer, or supplier, can be entered on separate sheets of paper and held in a ring-

RECEIPTS

Date	Invoice number	Details	Amount £
3.3.93	6042	Robinson	110.50
5.3.93	6029	Smith	79.54
9.3.93	6040	Jones	56.60
12.3.93	6041	Brown	201.17

PAYMENTS

Date	Cheque/ Voucher number	Details	Amount £
3.3.93	291196	Electricity	271.09
8.3.93	PC 37	Postage	2.16
11.3.93	PC 38	Railfares/ Newtown	21.40
15.3.93	291197	Barton's/ Typewriter repair	25.82

Figure 5.1 Cash book

binder, or folder, in alphabetical order. Figure 5.2 provides an example of a *sales ledger* sheet.

Invoices should always be sent out promptly once a job has been completed. If you delay, you give customers the impression that you are in no hurry to be paid. You do not need a special form for invoices. Your printed stationery will do. Each invoice should be numbered sequentially and should state, in the case of a business customer, the date the firm ordered the work to be done and their order number, if it has been provided. A copy of every invoice that you issue should be filed. You must do this, not only for your own reference but because you will need them for tax purposes later.

Where you are dealing with commercial firms, be sure to state on the invoice when you expect to receive payment. Few companies will settle within less than 30 days. Many will take 60 days or more, unless you stipulate otherwise. Business customers will also expect you to send a *statement*, as a reminder when payment becomes due. Make sure that Statements are sent out to reach customers a few days before the settlement date you have specified. Once again, you can use your printed stationery for this purpose.

5.6 INCOME TAX

As soon as you start the business, inform your local Inspector of Taxes and send him the P45 form you received from your last employer. His address can be found in the telephone directory, listed under Inland Revenue. You will be confirming your self-employed status and you will be taxed accordingly on the income you receive from the business.

As a self-employed person, you will be liable for all debts incurred by the business. This means that, should you fail, everything that you possess – house, car, furniture – could, as the result of a court order, be seized to pay your debts. In extreme cases, you could be made bankrupt.

There are, however, certain advantages to trading as a sole proprietor. The accounts that you are required to submit to the tax inspector should be a true statement of your trading activities for the period in question but they do not have to be pre-

Smith & Son

A/c no: .... Terms: 30 days

Folio no. ....

Date of invoice	Invoice number	Invoice value	Payment received	Date of payment

Figure 5.2 A sales ledger sheet

sented in any precise form. For a one-person business with a comparatively modest turnover, the taxman usually will be content with a Profit and Loss Account, showing gross earnings, the legitimate expenses incurred in the operation of the business and the net profit achieved. The tax of self-employed people is normally charged on a preceding-year basis. This can be an advantage to you because a period of several months may elapse from the end of your first year of trading before you are required to pay tax on any profits you have made. But the principal benefit of self-employed status for taxation purposes is that you are permitted to deduct what are described as *revenue expenses* from your profits that are 'wholly and exclusively incurred' in the operation of the business. This concession provides the self-employed person with an advantage not enjoyed by those who are salaried or wage-earning and who are taxed on PAYE.

Because this benefit exists, the Inland Revenue authorities are strict in their interpretation of what constitutes self-employed status. They are likely to question the validity of self-employment by individuals who appear to work principally for one client or customer, from whom they derive the bulk of their income. To avoid attracting any such suspicion, ensure that you do not put yourself in a position where you are operating your business at, or from, the premises of a client firm, or relying totally on having the use of equipment that belongs to a single customer. Where you have occasion to enter into a contractual arrangement with a client, make sure it is for services you are to render and not a *contract of service*. The safest way to operate your business for this and for many other reasons, is to have numbers of clients and not to have too many of your eggs in a single basket.

As a self-employed person, you will be liable to pay income tax on part of your earnings, if the income you obtain from working for yourself, when added to any other earnings you may have, exceeds your allowances. If your total earnings are small and you are doubtful about your liability, you should ask your local Inspector of Taxes for guidance.

Income tax will normally be charged on the taxable profits (takings less revenue expenses) that you have achieved in your accounting year, which is usually a period of twelve months. You are free to decide when your accounting year will start. It does not have to be a calendar year (January to December); nor the tax year which commences in April. But there is advantage if you so arrange your accounting year that it ends just after the beginning of the tax year because you gain some extra months between the time you actually make profits and when you have to pay the tax due on them.

Generally, the tax you are charged during the current tax year will be based on the taxable profits you made the previous year. You will be required to pay it in two instalments, half on 1 January and half on 1 July of the subsequent year.

The Inland Revenue specifies what may be deducted as business expenses. This includes goods for resale and materials bought for use in a business; advertising costs and delivery charges; the cost of postage, stationery, newspapers, books and magazines that relate to the information required in the running of the business. If you work from home, you are allowed to deduct a proportion of your telephone, heating, lighting, insurance and cleaning costs. You can deduct the cost of travel and accommodation incurred in making business visits. You can also deduct the entire running costs of a car if it is used solely for business purposes. If it is also used for private motoring, only a proportion of the costs is deductible. Should you take out insurance to cover business risks, such as third party public liability or indemnity, you can deduct the cost of the premiums you pay.

Capital expenditure is treated differently. You may not include it as a business expense for the year in which it was spent. The reasoning behind this is that capital equipment, such as vans, cars, machinery or scaffolding, ladders or computers, is not consumed by a business during its year of purchase. Tax relief is given for the cost of such items but it is spread over several years. This is done by pooling all capital purchases. The cost of each capital item that you purchase goes into the pool. You can claim what is called a writing down allowance of 25 per cent of the total value of the pool at the end of each of your tax accounting years. This sum is deducted from your profits for tax purposes. The amount you claim is also deducted from the value of the pool. Should you sell any item from the pool, the value of the pool will be further reduced by the amount of the proceeds of the sales.

Where the annual turnover of a business is below a stipulated figure, the Inland Revenue require only the figures for turnover, expenses and profit (what are described as 'three-line accounts'). Even if you are trading below this figure, however, you should still keep detailed records of your sales and purchases because the authorities are entitled, should they decide to do so, to ask for such details in support of the three-line accounts you have submitted.

For larger businesses, you should send to your tax office what is known as a Profit and Loss Account for the accounting year. This will show total receipts, total expenditure and the resulting profit (or loss) you have made. Figure 5.3 illustrates a typical layout for a Profit and Loss Account, including itemised entries for the principal items of expenditure.

Being self-employed, you will be under no compulsion to use the services of a qualified accountant to prepare your accounts for tax purposes: nor should you do so if you set up without capital and anticipate working to a very tight budget. Whilst it is true that the fees you would be charged by an accountant can be set against your taxable profits, these profits have to be earned.

JOHN SMITH *trading as SMITH'S GARDEN SERVICES*

Profit and Loss Account
year ending 30th June 1994

		£
Receipts		....
Less Expenses		
	Motor expenses	
	Advertising and Promotion	
	Stationery and Postage	
	HP interest (van)	
	Use of home	
		———— ....
Net Profit		....

Figure 5.3 Layout of a profit and loss account

In your first year of trading, you may do no more than break even once you have paid yourself a salary, and accountancy fees will be an overhead you could do without. As you progress and the business moves into profit, the help and advice of an accountant could make an important contribution to its further success.

In addition to your cash book and your sales and purchase ledgers, you should also file copies of all invoices, receipts and bank statements and retain used cheque books and bank paying-in slips, in case the Inland Revenue authorities should want to see them.

At the same time as you inform the taxman of your new status, you should do the same thing with the local office of the Department of Social Security, in respect to your National Insurance contributions. Where your earnings are over a certain figure, you will pay what is called Class 2 contributions. These are weekly flat-rate payments. In addition, you may have to pay Class 4 contributions which are calculated as a percentage of your profits. The simplest way to pay Class 2 contributions is via your bank by means of direct debit. Class 4 contributions are collected with your income tax payments.

5.7 USING YOUR HOME FOR BUSINESS

Technically, the use of any part of a private residence for business purposes involves a change of use for which planning consent is required. In practice, if the nature of the business you intend to conduct from your own home is such that it will not cause disturbance to your neighbours, your local authority will probably turn a blind eye. However, some trades inevitably cause nuisance to people living nearby because they create noise or smells. Another potential annoyance to other residents may occur if vans or large vehicles frequently park outside your home to deliver or collect goods. Similarly, where clients are in the habit of making visits, and in doing so occupy parking space hitherto used by your neighbours, your business could be considered a nuisance because it is causing an infringement of the amenities of others.

If you have doubts about these matters, ask you local planning department for their guidance. Where you are the owner-occupier of the property, obtain a copy of your deeds, to make sure that there are no restrictive covenants that could preclude your use of the premises for business purposes.

Once you use your home as a place of business, it is possible that you could endanger the legal liability cover that is incorporated in your home contents insurance policy, especially if visitors come to your home by way of business. Should anyone incur serious injury whilst on your premises and for which you could be held to be at fault, the legal costs and damages for which you could be liable would be terrifying. You should tell your insurers about the business you intend to operate on the premises. Make sure that they confirm to you *in writing* that you are covered on your contents policy. If not, you may have to pay a small extra premium.

Where you take on staff or have a partner working with you in the business, you will need *third party public liability insurance.* Another type of insurance cover you should certainly consider very seriously is indemnity insurance. This provides you with protection should a customer bring an action against you, claiming damages for harm that he or she claims to have been caused as a result of the service you have provided.

The list of potential risks you could incur in the running of your business and the variety of insurance cover available for your protection, appears virtually limitless. Apart from the cover you must have by law, you will need to apply a limit to the number of policies you take out. The best advice is to shop around to get the best available deals and to use the services of an insurance broker. He will generally offer reasonably impartial advice on the type of cover you will need for your kind of business. Being independent of any one insurance company, he should be able to arrange a policy for you best suited to your needs.

In recent years, legislation has been introduced to maintain the standards of certain services provided for the consumer. You will need a licence if you intend to provide financial advice to clients. The same applies if you decide to set up any form of employment agency. If your business involves the preparation of food at home for sale, you must abide by the statutory hygiene regulations and you should notify the environment health department of your local authority of your intentions *before* you begin operations.

The rents charged for commercial premises are generally high and you should use your own home, if possible, as your business base. Depending on your personal circumstances, however, this may not be convenient or desirable. Difficulties can occur in the use of one's home for the receipt of business mail. In most major towns, however, there are agencies that provide accommodation addresses specifically for independent business people faced with such problems. Some of them have interview rooms that can be hired on a daily or half-day basis as required. This can be useful if your line of business involves interviews with clients to be held on your ground rather than theirs. You can find your nearest agency by looking in *Yellow Pages*, under 'Accommodation Agencies – Business'.

An alternative venue for client meetings is a good-class hotel. Depending on the time of day, a quiet corner of a public lounge may suffice. But if you need somewhere more private to conduct business negotiations, most establishments have small conference rooms for hire, that will accommodate up to half a dozen people. Such facilities do not come cheaply but if their use enables you to clinch some rewarding deals, the outlay could be worthwhile.

5.8   YOUR BANK MANAGER

The theme of this book is self-help. It is made necessary because virtually all government and private sector schemes designed to provide financial assistance for the start-up of a small business require a proportion of the money to be found from the proprietor's personal resources. This slams the door in the face of someone like you, who it is assumed has no disposable capital sum.

A significant change has occurred with regard to borrowing within the last year or so. The have-it-now-pay-later attitude of the eighties has given way to far greater caution, in the light of thousands of house repossessions and business failures that have left owners facing mountainous debts. Not having any capital effectively prevents you from running a similar risk. But it also prevents you from receiving the benefit of much information and advice that inclusion in such schemes will often provide.

Self-help should not result in isolation. You should take every opportunity to obtain free guidance and specialised advice to assist you in working for yourself, wherever this is on offer. One possible source of advice and assistance is your bank. If your former employer paid your monthly salary into your bank account, you should make a point of seeing your branch manager, to explain why these regular receipts have been discontinued. Use the opportunity to tell him your future plans. The

response you get will depend very much on the outlook of the
manager and the view he takes of the long-term viability of the
venture. If you have done your homework and prepared a business plan, you should be able to outline your intentions in a positive and practical manner. Providing he likes the look of you and
takes a favourable view of your future prospects, he could be a
valuable contact. A well-disposed bank manager can be helpful
in offering advice and, at a practical level, in suggesting sales
leads to potential customers for your service, particularly if your
market includes locally based commercial firms who are also
customers of his bank. There is also the possibility that he may
even suggest a small facility, such as an overdraft of perhaps a
few hundred pounds, to tide you over until revenue from the
business starts to come in.

5.9   TRAINING AND ENTERPRISE COUNCILS

The income you receive from your business in its first year may
not necessarily be sufficient to enable you to maintain the life-
style to which you are accustomed. Indeed, it may prove to be
less than the dole money you would receive if you remained unemployed. It was recognition of this dilemma that motivated
the Government to introduce the old Enterprise Allowance
Scheme. For those registered as unemployed, who had a business idea considered viable, a grant of £40 per week was provided for a period of twelve months to help them get started.
Applicants had to put £1000 pounds of their own money into
the venture but this sum could, if necessary, be raised by means
of a loan.

In the light of experience, this blanket approach to resolving
the problem of new business start-up by the unemployed has
been superseded. The emergence of regionally based Training
and Enterprise Councils (TECs), known in Scotland as LECs
(Local Enterprise Councils), has provided a channel for assistance that is thought to be more closely related to the specific
needs of local areas.

Local authorities and local businesses have come together to
provide the funding for TECs and to supply training facilities

and commercial advice to those on the unemployment register who are anxious to start their own businesses. Schemes vary considerably in different parts of the country. In general terms, the original objective of the former Enterprise Allowance Scheme has been maintained. However, the new arrangements provide for closer scrutiny of the viability of new business proposals and the capability of candidates to develop them successfully.

Aspirants are initially screened for their personal suitability. They are required to produce a business plan and are given assistance in doing so. The plan is then considered by independent counsellors – usually experienced local business people – and an individually tailored scheme is devised to assist the setting up of the business. This is likely to include a period of training, help in obtaining start-up capital and a grant of money designed to sustain the applicant until the business is established. Broadly speaking, grants are in the region of £40–60 per week for a year, although the period may be extended in certain circumstances.

In order to qualify for consideration by your local TEC, you must have been registered unemployed for six weeks or be under personal notice of redundancy. You will need to be over 18 years of age and under 65. You must also be able to show that you will devote a minimum of 36 hours per week to the business.

The thinking that has inspired the amended arrangements is that the limited amount of public money available to the scheme should be directed where it will do the most good, in backing 'winners'. There is also very considerable emphasis being placed on the support for business ventures that, once established, will provide jobs in the local area. The intention, without doubt, is commendable. What may give rise to concern, however, is that administration of these schemes, including the vital initial screening of candidates, is conducted by officials appointed by the local authority. Whilst the dedication of such individuals is not in question, how qualified they are likely to be to pronounce on matters relating to enterprise and the possession of entrepreneurial flair, is another matter. No doubt a number of people, keen to work for themselves, whose business plans conform sufficiently to the norms laid down by their Town Hall, will pass through the mesh and will eventually benefit from the help they receive.

5.10   THE RURAL DEVELOPMENT COMMISSION

If you live in the English countryside or in a small town of less than ten thousand inhabitants, the Rural Development Commission could provide a source of advice and assistance. This is a government-funded agency, whose primary purpose is to encourage enterprise in the rural areas of England. These account for 20 per cent of the total national population, yet only one person in ten earns a living from agriculture. For this reason, the remit of the Commission excludes traditional rural activities, such as farming, forestry and horticulture, which are assisted by other agencies, to enable its resources to be directed specifically towards industrial and commercial development that will increase employment opportunities. Help is channelled through local offices situated throughout the country and encompasses such subjects as business management, marketing, rural tourism, premises and specialist skills.

If you have specific problems and need advice, your initial contact with the regional Business Adviser will be free of charge, although a negotiated fee will be charged for any subsequent consultations.

Loans and grants are obtainable from the Commission for approved business development but finance can only be made available to cover the difference between the costs involved in a project and that which an applicant can raise from other sources. Since you will, presumably, be operating without capital of your own, you will be unable to take advantage of this facility. Nevertheless, the advisory function undertaken by the Commission could be of benefit to you.

Useful Addresses

Alliance of Small Firms and Self-Employed People
33 The Green
Calne
Wiltshire SN11 8DJ
Tel: 0249 817003

Antiques Trade Gazette
17 Whitcomb Street
London WC2H 7PL
Tel: 071-930 7192

Association of Independent Computer Specialists
5 Bridge Avenue
Maidenhead
Berkshire SL6 1RR
Tel: 0628 35913

Books and Bookmen
43 Museum Street
London WC1A 1LY

Booksellers Association
Minster House
Vauxhall Bridge Road
London SW1V 1BA

British Agents Register
24 Mount Parade
Harrogate
North Yorkshire HG1 1BP
Tel: 0423 560608

British Decorators Association
45 Sheen Lane
London SW14
Tel: 081-876 4415

British Handknitting Association
PO Box CR4
Leeds LS7 4NA

British List Brokers Association
Springfield House
Princess Street
Bedminster
Bristol BS3 4EF
Tel: 0272 666900

Business In The Community
227a City Road
London EC1V 1LX
Tel: 071-253 3716

Campaign
22 Lancaster Gate
London W2 3LY
Tel: 071-402 4200

Craftsman Magazine
PSB Design and Print Consultants Ltd
PO Box 5
Lowthorpe
Driffield
North Humberside YO25 8JD
Tel: 0377 45213

Data Protection Registrar
Springfield House
Water Lane
Wilmslow
Cheshire SK9 5AX
Tel: 0625 535777

English Tourist Board
Thames Tower
Black's Road
London W6 9EL

Tel: 081-846 9000
Equipment Leasing Association
18 Upper Grosvenor Street
London W1X 9PB
Tel: 071-491 2783

Ethnic Minority Business Development Unit
City of London Polytechnic
Calcutta House
Old Castle Street
London E1 7NT
Tel: 071-283 1030

Federation of Small Businesses
140 Lower Marsh
London SE1 7AE
Tel: 071-928 9272

Geographical Magazine
1 Kensington Gore
London SW7 2AR

Highlands and Islands Enterprise
Bridge House
20 Bank Street
Inverness IV1 1QR
Tel: 0463 234171

HMSO
St Crispins
Duke Street
Norwich NR3 1PD
Tel: 0603 622211

History Today
83–84 Berwick Street
London WC1A 3PJ
Tel: 071-439 8315

Institute of Heraldic and Genealogical Studies
82 Northgate
Canterbury,
Kent
Tel: 0227 68664

Institute of Linguists
24a Highbury Grove
London N5 2EA
Tel: 071-359 7445

Institute of Management Consultants
32–33 Hatton Garden
London EC1N 8DL
Tel: 071-242 2140

Institute of Patentees and Inventors
Suite 505a
Triumph House
189 Regent Street
London W1R 7WF
Tel: 071-242 7812

Institute of Translation and Interpreting
318a Finchley Road
London NW3 5HT
Tel: 071-794 9931

Landscape Institute
Nash House
12 Carlton House Terrace
London SW1Y 5AH
Tel: 071-839 4044

London College of Fashion
20 John Princes Street
London W1
Tel: 071-629 9401

London and Provincial Antique Dealers Association
535 King's Road
London SW10 0SZ
Tel: 071-823 3511

Market Research Society
15 Northburgh Street
London EC1V 0AH
Tel: 071-490 4911

The Musician
239 Shaftesbury Avenue
London WC2H 8EH
Tel: 071-240 5749

Northern Consultants Association
Unit 1a
Mountjoy Research Centre
Durham DH1 3SW
Tel: 091-386 0800

Patent Office
Cardiff Road
Newport
Gwent NP9 1RH
Tel: 0633 814000

Rural Development Commission
  North Region
  Morton Road
  Yarm Road Industrial Estate
  Darlington
  Co.Durham DL1 4TE
  Tel: 0325 487123

  South Region
  141 Castle Street
  Salisbury
  Wiltshire SP1 3TP
  Tel: 0722 336255

East Region
18 Market Place
Bingham
Nottingham NG13 8AP
Tel: 0949 839222

West Region
Ullswater Road
Penrith
Cumbria CA11 7EH
Tel: 0768 65752

Small Business Agency for Northern Ireland
LEDU House
Upper Galwally
Belfast BT8 4TB
Tel: 0232 491031

Scottish Business in the Community
Romano House
43 Station Road
Corstorphine
Edinburgh EH12 7AF
Tel: 031-334 9876

Scottish Enterprise
120 Bothwell Street
Glasgow G2 7JP
Tel: 041-248 2700

Scottish Tourist Board
23 Ravelston Terrace
Edinburgh EH4 3EU
Tel: 031-332 2433

Small Business Bureau
46 Westminster Palace Gardens
Artillery Row
London SW1P 1RR
Tel: 071-976 7262

Society of Genealogists
14 Charterhouse Buildings
Goswell Road
London EC1M 7BA
Tel: 071-251 8799

Training and Enterprise Councils (*see your local Job Centre*)

Translators Association
Society of Authors
84 Drayton Gardens
London SW10 9SD
Tel: 071-373 6642

Welsh Development Agency
Pearl House
Greyfriars Road
Cardiff CF1 3XX
Tel: 0222 222666

Commonly-Used
Business Terms

Assets   Funds or properties owned by a business.

Bankruptcy   Insolvency – the inability to pay debts.

Benefit   A feature of a service or product that is
                      likely to have a distinct appeal to a cus-
                      tomer because it will satisfy a particular
                      need.

Broker   An individual or firm employed in the
                      negotiation of a commercial transaction
                      between other parties in the interests of
                      one of the principals.

Capital   The entire resources of a business, includ-
                      ing cash, stock, equipment and property.

Cash   Ready money.

Cash Book   A book of account in which day-to-day
                      receipts and payments of a business are
                      recorded.

Cash Discount   An amount deducted from the charge
                      made for a service, or for goods, as an
                      inducement to secure early payment by
                      the customer.

Cash Flow   The inward and outward flow of cash
                      experienced by a business during a speci-
                      fic period of time.

Commission	Remuneration, in the form of a percentage of the value, paid by a principal to an agent for arranging a sale, or a purchase, on his behalf.
Credit Terms	The period of time that is permitted for payment of goods or services that have been provided.
Customs and Excise	Department of the Civil Service responsible for the collection of Value Added Tax, among other duties.
Feature	A notable property of a service or a product that offers potential advantages to customers. Features only become *benefits* when they meet specific needs of a customer.
Fixed Costs	Expenses that remain unchanged despite variation in the output achievements of a business.
Goodwill	An intangible asset of a business based on its favourable reputation and the constancy of its customers.
Inflation	The rate of increase of prices for goods and services that are included in the Retail Price Index.
Interest	The annual charge, usually in the form of a percentage, that is applied by the lender and paid by the borrower of a capital sum.
Invoice	A document that sets out the details of a commercial transaction and is sent by the supplier to the purchaser of goods or

services, with an indication of when payment should be made.

Limited Company   A form of business where, in the event of insolvency, the liability of its directors is limited to the loss of the assets of the business, and their personal assets remain untouched.

Liquid Assets   Business assets that can be quickly converted into cash.

Loan Capital   Money borrowed by a business for a set period of time for which the rate of interest is fixed in advance.

Market Segment   A section of the market consisting of customers and potential customers who share similar needs which are distinct from the needs of those in other segments.

Market Share   A firm's sales, by volume, to a market, expressed as a percentage of the total volume of sales made to the market.

Market Research   Measures that are taken to identify and assess the market for services or products, its composition and current and future trends.

National Insurance   A scheme run by the Department of Social Service to provide payments to employed individuals during periods of illness or unemployment, as well as the state retirement pension. It is funded by contributions, based on a percentage of their earnings, by all those in work, which are augmented by contributions levied on employers.

Overdraft   The limit to which a bank will permit an individual customer to borrow without penalty, subject to status, at a variable interest rate based on an agreed percentage above the Minimum Lending Rate of the Bank of England. Unlike a loan, this facility can be withdrawn by the bank at any time.

Overhead   A *fixed cost* of a business.

Patent   Legal protection that provides the exclusive right to manufacture and sell a new product for a specified period of time.

PAYE   The pay-as-you-earn procedure that provides for the income tax and national insurance contributions of employees to be deducted by their employers from their wages or salaries and paid to the Inland Revenue authorities.

Schedule D   The Schedule of the Inland Revenue that sets out the permissible tax allowances applicable to the self-employed.

Variable Costs   Expenditure that varies in accordance with variation in the output achievements of a business.

Index